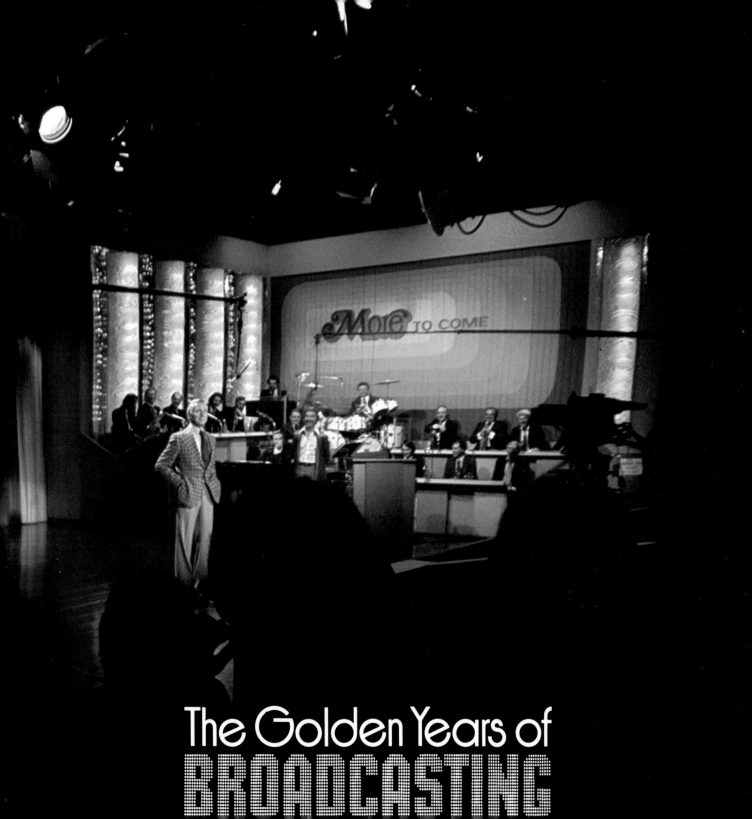

The Golden Years of
BROADCASTING

The Golden Years of
BROADCASTING

A Celebration of the First 50 Years of Radio and TV on NBC

by Robert Campbell

A Rutledge Book
Charles Scribner's Sons
New York

Fred R. Sammis: *Publisher*
John Sammis: *Executive Director*
Jeanne McClow: *Editor-in-Chief*
Allan Mogel: *Art Director*
Julianne deVere: *Production Director*
B. G. Murphy: *Editor*
Mimi Koren: *Editor*
Jeremy Friedlander: *Editor*
Pat Douglas: *Production Manager*
Jay Hyams: *Associate Editor*
Lee Hoeting: *Assistant Editor*
Elyse Shick: *Associate Art Director*
Eric Marshall: *Art Associate*
Susan Lurie: *Editorial Assistant*
Candida Pilla: *Editorial Assistant*

Robert Kasmire: *Special Consultant*

*Prepared and produced by Rutledge Books, a division of Arcata
Consumer Products Corporation, 25 West 43 Street, New York, N.Y.
10036. Published in 1976 by Charles Scribner's Sons, 597 Fifth
Avenue, New York, N.Y. 10017. Copyright 1976 in all countries of
the International Copyright Union by Rutledge Books and National
Broadcasting Company, Inc.*

Library of Congress Cataloging in Publication Data

Campbell, Robert, 1922-
    The golden years of broadcasting.

    1. National Broadcasting Company, inc. 2. Television programs
—United States—History. 3. Radio programs—United States—His-
tory. I. Title.
HE8689.8.C36 1976   384.54'06'573   76-19034
ISBN 0-684-14816-1

There are several ways to tell the story of NBC's first fifty years. This book is the result of a choice—to try to tell it primarily through the programs NBC has presented during those years, in the framework of the factors influencing broadcasting's development. This approach was selected because it is the service of broadcasting—the entertainment, news, and public affairs programs—with which the public is most concerned.

The history of NBC has also been shaped by many enterprising, talented, and dedicated people—the executives who have guided NBC through its growth and been responsible for its achievements. Except for one, David Sarnoff, the founder of NBC and of national broadcasting, their names do not appear in this book. The NBC story could have been told in terms of their contributions to the development of NBC and broadcasting in this country. That would have been an interesting book, too, but a different one.

CONTENTS

Foreword

Y̵ou could say that NBC and I sort of grew up together. I've been solid with them for over a quarter century on television, and for sixteen years before that on radio. And my, what a lot's happened since those early days! When the first big broadcast came on the air, back in the fall of 1926, I didn't pay much attention. I was already pretty well established as a vaudeville comedian. In 1929, the Radio-Keith-Orpheum office signed me for three years, to play theaters all over the country. Happily, I was quite successful. Every once in a while someone from Keith would come up and ask, "Would you go on the RKO *Theater of the Air?*" And I'd say, "Well, what for?" And then I'd turn to somebody and ask, "Where're we supposed to open next week? . . . Minneapolis?" I didn't think much about radio.

One of the greatest entertainment theaters in those days was the big Capitol, on Broadway in New York. It was a very smart, classy motion-picture house. A big band sat in the pit, and the pit itself would rise with the band playing, while singers and dancers performed on the stage. Then the pit would be lowered and the picture run. Finally I, or whoever was working that week, would come on and do a show. The Capitol is where Bing Crosby and I first teamed up, in 1932, with Abe Lyman's big orchestra. I was emcee. After Bing sang a few songs we would clown around together. I hate to remember the things we did back then that people thought were funny—like each holding out his hands, thumbs down, for the other to milk. I did very well at the Capitol. Every time I came back they gave me a $500 raise. After a while I was making $2,750 a week, really powerful money.

During this time, Major Bowes produced a radio show from the Capitol. It was a variety music show on Sunday mornings. Every time I played the Capitol, the Major would be after me to appear on his show. Naturally I was flattered the first time he invited me—until I found out the reason. Bessie Mack, his press secretary (Ted Mack's sister), asked me, "Fix up a routine you can do with the Major and send it over." But during the show, the Major took all the punch lines! After that, when I worked up a routine for the two of us, I secretly prepared punch lines on top of punch lines, and also ad-libbed a lot. We got a lot of laughs, and he enjoyed every minute of it.

Gradually people here and there would come up and say, "Hey! I heard you on that radio show the other day. Pretty good." A light went on, and I said to myself, "Yeah. Maybe there's something to this radio thing." And something else helped convince me. There wasn't a theater in the country that opened in the evening before 7:30. Why? Because they knew nobody was going to leave the house until after *Amos 'n' Andy*. Nobody.

The first time I actually appeared on the NBC network was as a guest on the Rudy Vallee program, a marvelous variety show, in the early thirties. I got $750 each time I was on, and I used to take the check around the corner and look at it. I didn't believe I could get that kind of money. I used to stuff the checks in my pocket and run. In 1934, I did the Bromo Seltzer show. But I wasn't exactly a surefire, guaranteed shoo-in on radio yet. Once, I auditioned for Heinz Honey and Almond Cream in New York. For insurance, I invited all my wife Dolores's relatives down from the Bronx because I thought they'd be my greatest audience. They all came down and sat in this little narrow studio and just stared at me, while I rattled off jokes. They didn't even think about the jokes, or laugh or applaud or anything. They just sat there. And I could tell they were thinking, "How is he getting away with it?" Well, I didn't. I was so bad I didn't get the show. Shortly after, I did land the Woodbury soap show, with Shep Fields and his famous Rippling Rhythm orchestra. I opened the show with a little sketch, a monologue, and we did extremely well for several years.

In September, 1937, I signed to do some pictures with Paramount, so I came out to Hollywood, where I've been ever since. I figured I could do my Woodbury monologue from the NBC studio here, which was then on Melrose. Our show followed the *Chase & Sanborn Hour*, which was *the* big show on radio at the time. It aired at eight o'clock Sunday night and practically everybody in the country listened to it. In those days, Sunday night *was* NBC. The Chase & Sanborn show featured the biggest names: Eddie Cantor, Kate Smith, all the stars. Edgar Bergen was the main attraction on the show. He was the star of the world. Two years earlier we had been in the Ziegfeld Follies together, in Philadelphia, and they couldn't use him. They figured they had

Bob Hope in 1935 (top) during an early radio broadcast. His very first appearance on NBC, a few years before, had been as a guest of the popular crooner Rudy Vallee (opposite). Still earlier, in vaudeville, Hope had begun what was to become a lifelong association and friendship with Bing Crosby (shown here in 1946).

too much show already. Then he went on the Vallee show and was a smash. So Walter Thompson (J. Walter Thompson of the big ad agency) hired him for Chase & Sanborn, and he was over the top and gone.

When we were getting ready to follow Bergen with my first remote monologue for the Woodbury show, I said to John Swallow, who was then head of NBC programs on the West Coast, "How's everything for Sunday?"

"Oh, fine," he said.

"Did you give out the tickets?"

"Oh. You want an audience?"

"Do I want an audience? My God, how can I crack a string of jokes without one?"

My studio was right across from Bergen's. NBC set up some ropes, and when the Chase & Sanborn show was over, the poor unsuspecting audience was corralled right into my studio. They stood there, looking up at me by the mike on the stage. Very few of them knew me, because I hadn't been in pictures and wasn't a real big hit on radio yet. I said, "Come in and sit down. Just laugh, and I'll explain the whole thing to you later." They sat down, puzzled. But they had just come from Bergen's show, so they were in a good mood. I did my monologue about the funny things that happened to me when I arrived in Hollywood and what was happening in the country. Basically, it was the same contemporary format I used in vaudeville—taken from the newspaper headlines. I did five minutes, we got quite a few laughs, and it all went off very well. After that, I had my own audience and didn't have to borrow from Bergen.

In 1938, I did my own show for Pepsodent. For about ten years before that, the Pepsodent show had been strictly Amos 'n' Andy. But like everything else in show business, the Fresh-Air Taxicab Company had finally run out of gas. I took over, and we had a real hit show, all the way until 1950. It was a lot of fun. And there were so many fine comedians around, all of whom became my dear friends: Groucho, George Burns, Fred Allen, and of course Jack Benny, who was one of my dearest friends. Working in radio was wonderful. You could just stand there in front of a radio audience, tell a joke, get a laugh, and then kiss the joke and get another laugh. When the show was over, I'd just walk out, toss the script in a wastebasket, and go right to the golf course. I didn't have to worry about makeup, costumes, or anything like that. It was something.

Radio was a special medium because everyone who was listening built his own fantasy, had his own illusion of what things looked like. When Amos 'n' Andy came on the air, you "saw" the Fresh-Air Taxicab Company. It was all set in your mind. You imagined it your way; I imagined it my way; someone else saw it his way. It was all an illusion, a marvelous illusion. Fibber McGee's closet was crammed full of everything he owned. In nearly every episode, he'd go to that closet for something—his hat, a fishing rod—and the moment he opened the door, all this junk would come falling out and you would hear a crazy racket. There would be a pause, but there was always a final something that dropped out: clump, clump—crash! Everyone listening in had an image of that closet and all the junk that was in it and what

Bob Hope calls it "the big show on radio at the time": Edgar Bergen and Charlie McCarthy with guest Clark Gable on the Chase & Sanborn Hour *in 1939 (opposite). NBC superstars Eddie Cantor, Al Jolson, Gracie Allen, and George Burns reunite in 1947.*

Among Bob Hope's dear friends and favorite comedians have been Jack Benny (top), shown at the wheel of his sputtering old Maxwell, and Fred Allen and wife Portland Hoffa (above). Among his favorite occupations, over the years, has been entertaining GIs all over the world: "the most exciting and emotional part of my whole life," says Hope. On one occasion during World War II, Bob turned up at a remote base, walked on stage, and quipped to the assembled GIs: "Greetings, fellow tourists."

the last thing to come out was. Whenever Jack Benny opened his vault, where he presumably kept his miserly millions, there would be a great clanking of chains, and you could just see that vault. *The Inner Sanctum* opened with a deep, mysterious voice, in an echo-chamber effect, saying very slowly: "Good evening, ladies and gentlemen. Welcome to—the inner sanctum." And then you'd hear what sounded like a four-ton steel door, on rusty hinges, squeak slowly open. It seemed to take forever, and the suspense was killing. But you could see that door, imagine it, and your imagination intensified with each show. Tuning in was like visiting and revisiting your own private fantasies. That was the beautiful thing about radio.

When World War II began, the Navy offered Bing Crosby and me the rank of lieutenant commander if we would sign with them. But FDR sent us a message telling us not to join *any* service. Just entertain. So we did. We entertained troops all over the world. Once, in Alaska, we stopped to refuel at a little spot in the middle of nowhere in the dead of night. A couple of GIs ran off and woke up the day shift. So Bing and I got up on a tree stump about four feet wide, used it as a stage, and did a fifteen- or twenty-minute show for about fifteen soldiers. Then we got in the airplane and zoomed off again. Well, I got into the feeling of entertaining the GIs. It became a commitment, and was very gratifying. In fact it was the most exciting and emotional part of my whole life, playing for those guys, because they were so appreciative and made such great audiences. I got into the habit of touring. Throughout World War II, and up until 1948 in fact, I originated my regular Pepsodent show from Army, Navy, and Marine bases all over the world. Our entertainment troupes went just about everywhere. Someone once figured that in that time we traveled more than a million miles entertaining over 10 million troops. After that, I started my Christmas custom of taking a group of Hollywood entertainers to military bases in different parts of the world each year, to put on a Christmas show for the folks back home.

In 1950, I signed a five-year contract with NBC to go into television. I did my first show Easter Sunday from the roof of the New Amsterdam Theater on Forty-second Street in New York. To do that, I defected from motion pictures. In those days, television and pictures were mortal enemies. The picture people said, "You're going to be sorry for this." But NBC offered me such a good deal, I just couldn't turn it down. Ever since, I've had good ratings and a good relationship with NBC. Television is a completely different scene from radio, and a much harder one. First of all, you have to *appear*. You can't just walk on and read from a script, the way we did on radio. You have to look good, which first of all means makeup. On radio, we could look awful. It was only the act that mattered. On TV, you have to know your material. You can look at the idiot cards once in a while, as a reminder. But you can't be glancing at them too much because the audience will know. So you have to rehearse, really get your material together, force yourself to be natural.

The show's ratings were good from the start, and maybe that was bad. I was having fun, and I thought, "Gee. People are lucky and can see me now, just like it used to be in vaudeville, instead of just hearing me the way it was on radio." You get a kind of lush feeling when the ratings are high. You tend to coast, thinking, You're doing fine, so why rock the boat? I was in for a rude awakening. We have a

guest house at my place. About the time I signed my first NBC television contract, a friend of mine, Bones Hamilton, moved in. He had a little baby. And every time the baby cried, he'd point to my bedroom window and say, "Shh. Bob Hope's asleep." That was a weapon he used with the kid. In 1952, I was going to do a show from Cleveland, my hometown. The kid was three years old by then. So they sat him in front of a set to watch me. When I came on, they said to the kid, "That's Bob Hope." And the kid said, "Shh. Don't wake him." The kid was right. I was asleep.

The next day the Cleveland papers said, "This is Bob's hometown. Why would he come to his hometown and do a show like this?" It gave me a hell of a hangover when I read that. That's the kind of thing that can jolt you a little. So we scrapped everything and started over again. We learned to say, "What can we do now? What's different?" I don't ever again want to give anyone a reason to say, "Oh, that's just the same old Bob Hope."

Carrying a whole show is tough. And real comedy talent is a very rare thing, especially now that we don't have that terrific incubator we once had, called vaudeville. Vaudeville was great training because we did three or four shows a day. All kinds of shows: supper clubs, theaters, honky-tonks. It was a constant contest to see who survived. It was a great experience because it made you very resourceful about how to do things, how to sense the chemistry of an audience, and how to handle people. It was out of that background that George Burns and Jack Benny and Fred Allen and I came. You look around today and wonder: Where is NBC going to get new talent, now that vaudeville's dead? The amazing thing is, nearly every year a new face

appears. All of a sudden we have Jonathan Winters, who's wonderful. Then there's Freddie Prinze, really delightful. Out of nowhere comes Flip Wilson. Then John Byner pops up. And Tony Orlando, he's very bright. And of course there are all those crazy people on *NBC's Saturday Night,* a show I love. So these people must come from somewhere. We still have nightclubs. And there are small television stations, and college shows, and workshops. A lot of talent comes out of Las Vegas, too.

So I'm optimistic about the future. I've watched this industry grow from a few rinky-dink radio studios to a whole national institution that brings entertainment to millions and millions of people. And the whole news-gathering operation, from all over the world, is tremendous. A couple of years ago, we were visiting some friends in Green Bay, Wisconsin. We had a few days off, so they gave us their cottage in Egg Harbor, a little resort town farther up the bay. In the evenings we'd walk around this little town, looking in windows. Everybody was watching the Carson show. It reminded me of the old days when *Amos 'n' Andy* was so popular. Back then, you could walk down the street in the summertime and hear that show on everybody's radio.

Television is the greatest therapy ever invented. For many people, especially housewives, it's an all-day companion. They turn on that tube and go about their housework. Then, the kids take over when they come home. Whoever rules the knob, television is the greatest. Who would have thought that one day we'd have a motion-picture theater right in our own home? You can just pull up the chairs, put your popcorn on the side, and there you are. It's amazing. I love it. And I'm fortunate to be part of the action.

BOB HOPE

A Radio Music Box **Radio**

As recently as our grandparents' time, the airwaves were silent. With the exception of a few men, no one expected them to be otherwise. Those were the days of what is now referred to nostalgically as "small-town America." A worldwide communications network offering radio and television would have seemed idle fantasy.

What did people do with themselves for entertainment? They went on picnics. They went to band concerts in the park. They saw, occasionally, a traveling theater group. By far the biggest event, in summer or early fall, was the arrival of the circus in town—Ringling Brothers or Barnum and Bailey or the Hagenback-Wallace. There was a lot of small-town America to cover, and the circuses went to the people rather than the other way around.

Occasionally, once a year perhaps, a family would actually venture out of town, piling into the Ford tourer, the LaSalle, or a snorting Maxwell like Jack Benny's for a day in the faraway big city—Wilmington, Wichita, Walla Walla. Over winding, two-lane roads, a trip that today would take forty-five minutes was then a two-and-a-half- or three-hour ride with, perhaps, a flat to fix along the way.

Local newspapers also made some contact with the "outside world," using the wire services, which transmitted news over telegraph lines. Nevertheless, the main news source was the Sunday paper from the local metropolis: the *Baltimore Sun,* the *Chicago Tribune,* the *St. Louis Post Dispatch.* To kids, the papers brought the funnies. For the whole family, there were also magazines. People waited anxiously for the mailman to bring *Cosmopolitan* or *The Saturday Evening Post.* In the latter case, West Coast readers had quite a wait. Copies were shipped to the coast by boat, via the Panama Canal.

Those were relatively placid times. Progress was comprehensible. Then, on December 12, 1901, at St. John's, on the frosty, windswept coast of Newfoundland, an event occurred that signaled the beginning of a revolution in communications, a revolution that would ultimately increase incredibly social awareness and bring about great social change.

On that December day, at the turn of the century, a dapper and aristocratic inventor, Guglielmo Marconi, launched a box kite into the coastal winds, playing out line as it climbed higher and higher. The kite trailed an array of thin wires, acting as a primitive receiving antenna. At a prearranged time that afternoon, the Italian put on earphones and began to listen. He heard a faint signal, three dots, the letter *S* in Morse code. The signal had traveled through the air a distance of more than 2,000 nautical miles, roughly following the fiftieth parallel from a similar station Marconi had earlier established at Cornwall, on the southern tip of England.

No sooner had the vast reach of Marconi's "wire-less" invention been established than permanent transatlantic stations were set up in quick succession. One, at South Wellfleet on Cape Cod, featured twenty wooden masts, 200 feet high, supporting antenna wires at the top and set in the sand circling the station. Dubious Cape Codders said the first good nor'easter would wipe out the masts. It did. Marconi replaced them with four 250-foot towers, anchored in cement. They held.

Producing wireless signals that could cross the Atlantic and be heard at the other end required outsized power-generating equipment, not the small, fast-acting key a tradi-

Clockwise from below: The rooftop antenna of AT&T's station WEAF, overlooking lower Manhattan in 1922; a radio-equipped cart on the boardwalk at Atlantic City, N.J., where strollers could listen in on "the world's first real broadcast" in 1921, at 25¢ a round; a pair of charming entertainers, Dorothy and Lillian Gish, in an NBC studio; two dapper gentlemen who started it all—David Sarnoff and Guglielmo Marconi.

tional telegrapher used to tap out messages carried on wire, sending a hundred words and more a minute. Power for early wirelesses was provided by a massive rotor with a three-foot spark gap. The key was referred to as the "pump handle." It could send about seventeen words a minute, with vigorous pumping.

On the flat and almost featureless sands of Cape Cod, the early wireless stations formed natural targets for lightning. One hit fused a coal bucket to the stove. Another shattered a wooden stool. One operator was killed and a second was knocked right out of his shoes. Despite such mishaps, the development of wireless continued.

President Theodore Roosevelt, fascinated by the new invention, sent a message to the king of England. Edward VII responded promptly. With growing transatlantic message traffic, the era of the wireless became a fact of life. Predictably, equipment grew smaller, simpler, and more powerful, until a wireless operator aboard a ship at sea or at a station ashore could rival telegraphers in the rapid transmission of Morse code.

An upshot of these pioneering operations was the Marconi Wireless Telegraph Company of America. One operator of the fledgling company was a young Russian emigrant of considerable talent, genius, and foresight: David Sarnoff. He was ultimately to become the founder of NBC. At the age of fifteen, in 1906, Sarnoff was hired by the Marconi company as an office boy. His gifts were so apparent that within two years he was promoted to full-fledged operator at the isolated and lonely Marconi station at Siasconset, on the eastern tip of Nantucket Island. With improved salary came extra time to study. Ambitious and in a hurry to get ahead, the young man had become an omnivorous reader and devoured the station's excellent technical library. Shortly afterward, he began night courses in technical engineering.

Following an eighteen-month stint as operator on several ships, Sarnoff took over a Marconi-owned station on top

Early manifestations of the "radio music box": portable field equipment, including a large loudspeaker used by WEAF in 1922 (opposite); a promotional photograph suggesting (by the handsome cabinetwork) that the radio could go with the living room furniture, though the lady looks dubious (top) a pioneer one-tube receiver, the "Aerola and the first of all RCA portable radio receivers (far right).

of the John Wanamaker department store in New York. Like some other businessmen of the day, the enterprising Wanamakers saw value in Marconi's invention. They put it to use for fast communications with their Philadelphia branch and also for receiving direct reports from Paris on fashion trends, thereby getting a jump on their competition.

Sarnoff had become such a skilled telegrapher that other operators could actually recognize a distinctive flair and touch to the signals his sensitive fingers produced as they rapidly tapped out messages on a wireless key. He had what was known as a "wireless fist."

On the night of April 14, 1912, David Sarnoff picked up an incredible message in his little shack atop the great store: "S.S. *Titanic* ran into iceberg—sinking fast." The new White Star liner, by far the largest ship built at the time and only on its maiden voyage from England to America, had been widely billed as truly unsinkable. The impossible had happened. An iceberg had sliced a 300-foot-long cut in the side of the vessel just below the waterline.

The *Titanic*'s distress signals were picked up by a number of vessels, including the *Carpathia,* a Cunard liner nearby, which began rushing to the rescue, and the *Titanic*'s sister ship, the *Olympic,* which was about 500 miles away. Of all the ships in the area, the *Olympic* had by far the most powerful wireless. It therefore became the relay station on that memorable night, and it was the *Olympic*'s wireless that Sarnoff was listening in on. As the extent of the calamity gradually became apparent, the fate of the more than 2,200 passengers and crew grew into a matter of worldwide concern. Some of the most notable people of the era were aboard for that stylish maiden voyage. Reporters, relatives, and the curious descended on Wanamakers, and the police had to put a guard around the store.

For three nights and three days David Sarnoff stuck to his post. President Taft ordered all other wirelesses on the East Coast off the air to keep Sarnoff's channel to the *Olympic* free of interference. Sarnoff's tour of duty paralleled that of the *Carpathia*'s operator, who was patiently relaying, via the *Olympic*, the names of the mere 705 survivors, who had been plucked from the icy North Atlantic, along with official messages concerned with the tragedy. It was a herculean, time-consuming task because each name had to be spelled out, letter by letter, in Morse code. The problems of relay were compounded by static, radio fade, and other forms of interference. Yet the list of survivors that Sarnoff slowly compiled, according to Walter Lord (author of *A Night to Remember*), was remarkably accurate, even down to the correct spelling of names.

The *Titanic* disaster firmly established the reliability and potential importance of wireless, and engineers and inventors began to develop ways of increasing its versatility. If simple dot-dash signals could be transmitted over thousands of miles, why not more complex signals as well? The vibrations of music are just such signals. So are those of the human voice. Within three short years after the *Titanic* went down, the problems of transmitting both voice and music by wireless had been solved. Radio was born.

David Sarnoff, assistant traffic manager for the Marconi company, wrote a memorandum to Edward J. Nally, the general manager, proposing a device that he referred to as "a radio music box" and outlining a plan of development that he believed "would make radio a household utility." He suggested that such a device could carry lectures, music, major national events, baseball scores, and other matters of

interest into the home, and that these reports could be carried on several frequencies, giving the listener a choice of programs.

By the end of World War I, the potential of radio was stirring interest in a variety of quarters. Other stores had followed the Wanamaker lead and installed communications systems to link their branches together. The United Fruit Line had equipped its fleet with radio so that ships could be immediately dispatched to profitable ports. Companies involved in the electrical equipment field (General Electric, Westinghouse, American Telephone & Telegraph) saw in radio a possible extension of their manufacturing operations and built experimental stations. Amateur radio stations across the country grew overnight like mushrooms.

Programming, of course, was spotty. The early stations went on the air sporadically, in many cases an hour or so after supper. A broadcast might consist of Mama playing the piano while Sis sang popular songs, such as "There's a Long, Long Trail Awinding," "My Little Grey Home in the West," or "I'm Forever Blowing Bubbles." A Westinghouse engineer, Frank Conrad, set up an experimental station in his garage with the call letters 8XK, played phonograph records on the air, and inadvertently became what was, most probably, the world's first disc jockey. 8XK shortly

Music, both classical and popular, became a staple of radio fare from the very inception of NBC, and three notable musicians of the day who appeared on the network's inaugural broadcast in the fall of 1926 are shown here. Vincent Lopez (left) came on the air with his society orchestra in a remote pickup. So did Ben Bernie (opposite). In this photograph of Bernie, taken in the early 30s, the famous orchestra leader sports a pair of natty elevated shoes, a highly pin-striped suit, and a roll-brim felt fedora, all of which were the "latest thing" at the time. For the big broadcast, on the classical side, conductor Walter Damrosch (above) led the New York Symphony. In subsequent years his Music Appreciation Hour introduced millions of Americans to classical works they had never heard before.

More stars of NBC's inaugural broadcast of November 15, 1926:
Will Rogers (right) and the famous vaudeville team of
Weber and Fields (opposite). One of the classic "inventions" of
early radio was the serial drama, and one of the earliest
dramas was One Man's Family (below), with Bernice Berwin as
Hazel, J. Anthony Smythe as Father Barbour, and Minetta
Ellen as Mother. It ran 15 minutes a day, like other such dramas.

thereafter became KDKA-Pittsburgh, one of the earliest and
most famous commercial stations. Owned by Westinghouse, its "studios" were moved from Conrad's garage to a
coatroom in the company's electric-meter factory. The coats
acted as baffles to muffle stray noises that otherwise would
have been picked up by the microphone along with the
program itself. At about the same time, a group of companies consolidated their individual radio efforts and formed
the Radio Corporation of America. RCA acquired the Marconi company.

With so many stations, there was a scramble to acquire
frequencies and call letters to identify them. Some of the
early labels actually meant something. WGN in Chicago,
owned by Colonel Berty MacCormick's newspaper, the Tribune, stood for "World's Greatest Newspaper." WGBS in
New York was the station of "Gimbel Brothers' Store."
WGEC in Schenectady belonged to the General Electric
Company. WINS, also in New York, was named for International News Service.

On July 2, 1921, RCA borrowed what was then the
world's most powerful radio transmitter, to broadcast the
world heavyweight title fight between Jack Dempsey and
George Carpentier of France. The transmitter belonged to
the United States Navy. The arrangement was facilitated by
Undersecretary of the Navy Franklin Delano Roosevelt.
Dempsey's win in New Jersey was heard by avid listeners
throughout the New York area.

Local newspapers carried little or no news of early radio experiments, suspecting rightly that sinister competition was being born. But Reuters, the British news agency,
called the Dempsey-Carpentier fight "the world's first real
broadcast."

The following year, as general manager of RCA, Sarnoff
wrote a memorandum to the chairman of GE, one of the RCA
parent companies, predicting that broadcasting was des-

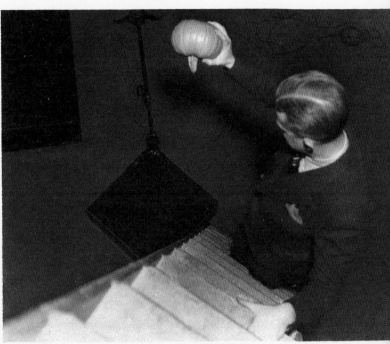

The indispensable ingredients that helped imaginations run amok in the dear old days of radio: the sound effects man and his marvelous inventions. At far left is a jail cell door that could clang shut on a malefactor. A "squeaking factor" could be added to simulate dark doings in a castle dungeon. At the center of the picture, on the floor, is a massive chain draped over a metal brace; next to it is an array of gears that produced various grinding noises when turned at different speeds. These two devices, used in combination, could sound like a ship's anchor being weighed, a clanking drawbridge being lowered, or Jack Benny's safe being opened. The effects man, script in hand, stands ready to open a more ordinary door on cue. It could also be slammed, squeak shut slowly, or, with the mike in close, yield the alarming sound of an intruder slowly turning the doorknob or forcing the latch. At the rear is a console for playing recorded sounds. NBC had a library of several thousand records of almost everything imaginable: train whistles, galloping horses, squealing tires, swamp noises, all sorts of firearms, city traffic, whirring presses, birdcalls, animal sounds, and so on. A particularly gruesome studio effect, that of a body falling to the ground, was produced by dropping a pumpkin from a stepladder (above). A fairly green melon evoked a fall of a few floors; an overripe one suggested that the victim had plunged (possibly with the aid of a shove) from a cliff, hotel, office, or even a skyscraper.

27

tined to become a quality public service and that a specialized organization would be needed to provide it on a national scale. "The broadcasting station will ultimately be required to entertain a nation," he added.

By 1923, WEAF, a New York station owned by American Telephone & Telegraph, had instituted regular radio programming, including a weekly news broadcast by the noted commentator H. V. Kaltenborn. The following year, a dozen stations, similarly linked, carried parts of the GOP convention. And in 1925, twenty-six stations carried Coolidge's inaugural address. These early hookups, largely under the aegis of AT&T, represented a natural interest on the part of the big telephone company. If the idea of a radio network should prove to be commercially feasible, programs would be carried on its long-distance lines, which could be profitable to the company. But as the prospects evolved, it became apparent that a considerable amount of attention would have to be paid to getting program materials on the air, and AT&T felt that going into the entertainment business was not exactly its line of work. It sold WEAF to RCA (the

station later became NBC), where some very definite programming ideas were ready to go on the air.

It happened on November 15, 1926, from 8:00 P.M. to well past midnight, in the grand ballroom of the old Waldorf Astoria Hotel at Thirty-fourth Street and Fifth Avenue, in New York City. A thousand guests turned out in evening clothes for the inaugural broadcast of the National Broadcasting Company. Twenty-five stations in twenty-one cities, most of them charter affiliates, carried the New York program, which reached as far west as Kansas City. And what a show it was! There were opera stars like the great Metropolitan Opera baritone Titta Ruffo. Mary Garden, one of the most famous sopranos of the era, was picked up remote from Chicago to sing "Annie Laurie" and "My Little Grey Home in the West." Walter Damrosch led the New York Symphony, Alfred Stoessel the city's Oratorio Society. There was the big Goldman Band. There were remote pickups of four of New York's celebrated society orchestras: Ben Bernie, Vincent Lopez, B. A. Rolfe, and George Olsen. Weber and Fields, the renowned vaudeville team, provided laughs. Will Rogers was

Creating a mood of mystery or mayhem required sincere emoting to augment the sound effects. Though it was all quite invisible, a zealous NBC still photographer staged a mock slaughter of the Lights Out *cast (opposite) and a dramatically lit conference on* Ellery Queen *between Mikki (Marion Shockley), Sgt. Velie (Ted de Corsia), and Ellery (Carleton Young, with his back to the camera).*

29

picked up remote from Independence, Kansas, to poke fun at American politicians and other public targets, evoking knowing chuckles from all within earshot of a receiver. It was estimated that more than 2 million radios were tuned in for the big broadcast, which came across with various levels of infuriating static, depending on where the listeners were located.

The idea was such a success that, by the beginning of the following year, NBC was able to execute a second of Sarnoff's ideas. NBC split programming between two separate networks, called for convenience the red and the blue networks. Each offered a different program content, which gave the listeners a choice. By 1941, these two networks effectively blanketed the country. There were 103 blue subscribing stations, 76 red, and 64 supplementary stations using NBC programs. In general, the blue network programs leaned toward cultural offerings: music, drama, commentary. The red featured comedy and similar forms of entertainment. Eventually, the Federal Communications Commission ruled that no organization could own more than one network, so NBC sold the blue complex. It became the American Broadcasting Company.

The evolution of radio ended the isolation of small-town America. Instead of going to the city, people heard from it—on the radio. For only a dollar, approximately, you could buy a simple crystal set and earphones and pick up one, perhaps two, stations. The quality was quite poor, and sometimes you got nothing but static. Listening improved at night, though, and as transmitters grew more powerful and receivers more sensitive, the world of radio expanded. After dark, radio waves tend to bound incredible distances. Listeners can often pick up, much to their astonishment and delight, cities a thousand miles away and more. To the early listener, the experience was mind-boggling. All sorts of ideas, places, people, and experiences, things Americans had heard about vaguely if at all, added a new dimension to country living.

Daytime drama began early in the Midwest and acquired the handle "soap opera" because the early "soaps" were just that: short commercials for soap products, with an added touch of entertainment. A professor at Northwestern University suggested that the commercials would be more appealing if they were actually separated from small dramatic situations. The upshot was the fifteen-minute daytime series: *Road of Life, Ma Perkins, Portia Faces Life, Stella Dallas, Vic and Sade,* and many others.

Later in the day, clustered just before the dinner hour, came another of radio's most memorable achievements: the fifteen-minute adventure and mystery shows for children. Today, they provide endless quiz games for trivia buffs, just as the Sherlock Holmes stories do, such as: What was the first name of Little Orphan Annie's guardian? (Oliver "Daddy" Warbucks) What was the name of the Green Hornet's superfast automobile? (The Black Beauty) Over the years, these shows grew increasingly realistic and dramatic, thanks in large measure to the sound-effects man, whose efforts dramatically heightened tension as young people (and eavesdropping adults, too) listened, imaginations running amok, to such sinister sounds as the slowly squeaking door, shots fired in the night, the squishing and croaking of a swamp at midnight, the squealing tires of the getaway car, the crackling flames of the threatening fire.

There was *The Shadow*, who in "reality" was Lamont Cranston. In the Orient, he had learned a secret power: "to cloud men's minds." The only one who knew his identity was his lovely companion, Margo Lane. And there was the deep, resonant voice (honed to perfection in later years by Orson Welles), with its famous refrain: "The weed of crime bears bitter fruit. Who knows what evil lurks in the hearts of men. The Shadow knows! Ahhahahaha!" Aside from Daddy Warbucks (the supercapitalist war profiteer), *Little Orphan Annie* had other potent allies, all associates of Daddy. And they were quick to dispense vengeance. There was the giant Punjab, who could break a villain's neck with one arm. There was the slim, sinister, and appropriately named Asp, who could always be depended upon for a swift, sure, silent rub out—which usually took place offstage, leaving even more to the imagination, as the listener wondered how the execution was managed. The Asp never said; but you knew for sure that the other person would never be heard from again. Other heroes had other allies. *The Lone Ranger* had his trusty Indian scout, Tonto. And *The Green Hornet* (who in "reality" was Britt Reid, crusading newspaper editor) had his faithful Japanese valet, Kato. These programs, which kept kids riveted to the radio from about five to six o'clock each weekday evening, alarmed certain adults, who felt the programs incited violence in the young.

Like *The Shadow*, many of the programs had well-known opening lines: "A cloud of dust—a galloping horse with the speed of light—the Lone Ranger!" "Jack Armstrong, the All-American Boy!" "Buck Rogers—in the Twenty-Fifth Century!" (The last accompanied by the lovely Wilma Deering and the cerebral scientist Dr. Huer.) Music was a hallmark of many shows, too. *The Lone Ranger* came on with the *William Tell Overture*, complete with galloping hooves. *The Green Hornet* opened with the *Flight of the Bumblebee*, suggesting great excitement to come. Many

Charles Lindbergh (above) on the air shortly after his historic solo flight to Paris in The Spirit of St. Louis in 1927. Clockwise from right opposite: "The Happiness Boys," Billy Jones and Ernie Hare, exude happiness into an old radio mike; Lucille Wall, Karl Swenson, and Colleen Ward during a tense moment on Lorenzo Jones; a bright bit of repartee over the table during Don McNeill's Breakfast Club, another durable contribution of the Chicago school to early radio days.

PRESS RADIO ELECTION RETURNS AS BROADCAST
BY THE NATIONAL BROADCASTING COMPANY
TOTAL ELECTORAL VOTES - 531 - NECESSARY TO ELECT - 266 -

ROOSEVELT-GREEN   LANDON - AMBER

programs had their own original music, often with the commercials built in:

She and Sandy make a pair.
　　They never seem to have a care.
Cute little she—
　　It's Little Orphan Annie.

They're crispy, they're crunchy
　　The whole day through.
Jack Armstrong never tires of them
　　And neither will you!
So just buy Wheaties,

the best breakfast food in the land!

Once you try it, you'll stay by it.
　　Tom Mix says it's swell to eat.
Jane and Jimmy, too, say it's best for you,
　　Ralston cereal can't be beat.

When Charles Lindbergh returned to Washington from his triumphant transatlantic flight to Paris, in 1927, four NBC correspondents covered the event: one at the Navy Yard where the cruiser carrying the famed aviator docked, one in the Capitol dome, one on Pennsylvania Avenue for the parade, and a fourth at the top of the Washington Monument to

Moments in the news. NBC's display of election night returns in 1936 (opposite), when Franklin Roosevelt swamped Alf Landon and took every state except Maine and Vermont. There were only 531 electoral votes at the time. The board was set up in front of the RCA building; the viewers are blurred by the time exposure. FDR (above) gives one of his famous fireside chats. Actor Paul Douglas (left) in his early days as a young broadcaster.

Clockwise from left: The greatest "Mammy" singer of all time, Al Jolson, who came to NBC in 1928, was still belting them out 20 years later when this picture was taken; on the Town Hall Tonight show, John Brown, Portland Hoffa (Fred's wife), and the wryly wonderful Fred Allen himself take the radio audience for a visit to the imaginary and hilarious town of Bedlamville; "So long until tomorrow," newscaster Lowell Thomas's characteristic sign-off, was familiar to millions for nearly half a century; one of NBC's most famous sportscasters, Clem McCarthy (with staff man Hal Totten on the right), at the ringside in Chicago for the 1936 fight between an upcoming Joe Louis and one Charlie Retzlaff, a journeyman heavyweight whom Louis dispatched in the first round. The following year Joe Louis defeated Jimmy Braddock to become one of the greatest world heavyweight champions of all time.

wrap it all up. It was a big day. A year later, NBC began coverage of national political conventions, campaigns, and elections, which had a profound impact on the democratic process by bringing millions more voters to the polls. When Al Smith lost to Herbert Hoover, some felt it was partly due to his "East-Side New York" accent. Four years later, Franklin D. Roosevelt's aristocratic and magnetic radio voice would in turn contribute to Hoover's defeat. "We have nothing to fear but fear itself," FDR told the nation on taking office. In the years that followed, his famous "Fireside Chats" helped to assure his tenure at the White House.

In many ways, what became news was partially determined by where radio could go. There was a first broadcast from an airplane in flight, a first from a submarine, a first from the French balloonist Auguste Piccard's gondola drifting ten miles up over the Dakotas, a first from William Beebe's deep-sea bathysphere a half mile down in the ocean. Gradually, the radio newscaster became as ubiquitous a presence on the national and world scene as the reporters who covered the same beats for the newspapers, magazines, and wire services. As the clouds of war gath-

ered over Europe in the late 1930s, both the numbers and assignments of radio reporters increased dramatically.

Starting with the coast-to-coast broadcast of the Rose Bowl game of 1927, sporting events became a radio staple. That same year, the red and blue networks tied in with a number of independent stations to broadcast the second Tunney-Dempsey fight from Soldiers' Field in Chicago. It was heard across the country via sixty-nine radio stations. Two years later came the first network broadcast of a Kentucky Derby. During the twenties and thirties, NBC broadcast the World Series many times. The network also covered major football games, golf tournaments, and the Olympics at Los Angeles in 1932 (which discovered Babe Didrickson) and in Berlin in 1936 (where Jesse Owens, a black American, proved to be the fastest man on earth, much to the disgust of Adolf Hitler).

In his 1922 memorandum to the chairman of GE, David Sarnoff had noted that "the broadcasting station will ultimately be required to entertain a nation." Whether or not he foresaw that radio, along with the movies, would soon kill vaudeville—which had been the forum for many singers,

Clockwise from left: Eddie "Banjo Eyes" Cantor on the air in 1932; one of the great clowns, Ed Wynn (father of actor Keenan Wynn), in his memorable role of the Texaco Fire Chief who, according to his cap, dispensed "gasoloon"; a very young and somewhat lascivious-looking Jack Benny; a zany Red Skelton with some outlandish uppers breaks up announcers Ned Le Fevre and Rod O'Connor; the host of the Jimmy Durante Show, the Schnozzola himself, breaks into an exuberant song with a very lovely lady guest from Hollywood, actress Greer Garson.

The original and authentic "funny girl," Fanny Brice (above) played a
very funny "Baby Snooks" on radio. Earlier, as a showgirl, she had
had a warm, intense, and ultimately doomed love affair with mobster Nicky
Arnstein, which provided the plot for the movie Funny Girl, in which
Barbra Streisand played Fanny. Opposite: Gertrude Berg, the warmhearted
mother on The Rise of the Goldbergs, a popular serial for many years.

jugglers, stand-up comics, and other entertainers until the late twenties—that was exactly what happened. NBC signed up Eddie Cantor in 1926 and Al Jolson ("The Jazz Singer") two years later. The parade of vaudeville-trained names to radio is legendary, and the former vaudevillians became a kind of national property: Rudy Vallee, Fred Allen, Jack Benny, Ed Wynn, Groucho Marx, Bob Hope, Jimmy Durante, Bing Crosby, Red Skelton, Fibber McGee and Molly, Edgar Bergen and Charlie McCarthy, George Burns and Gracie Allen, to name only a few. They had their own shows, appeared on each other's shows, and sometimes engaged in mock feuds.

Though most comedy and variety shows originated with NBC, not all did. One notable exception, called *Sam 'n' Henry,* came on the air locally in Chicago over station WGN in 1926. The show was about the trials and tribulations of a somewhat pompous black man, the proprietor of a Chicago taxicab company, and his much put-upon driver. It was the creation of two very talented white men, Freeman Fisher Gosden and Charles J. Correll, who not only wrote the show but acted it. Two years later, the program moved to NBC's Chicago affiliate, WMAQ, as *Amos 'n' Andy,* with Gosden playing Amos and Correll as Andy. The two versatile writer-actors also played all the other roles in their imaginary scenario: the mellow-voiced Kingfish, head of the local lodge known as The Mystic Knights of the Sea, Brother Crawford, an eminent member of the lodge, and Madam Queen, who had her hat set on marrying Andy, a situation that led to some hilarious near-misses as Andy twisted this way and that to avoid entrapment. In 1929, *Amos 'n' Andy,* sponsored by Pepsodent, went on the NBC network, settling into a fifteen-minute time slot at 7:00 P.M. The impact was stupefying, to say the least. For years, virtually a whole nation stopped whatever it was doing to tune in to the show, which opened on the melodic strains of a tune called "A Perfect Song." For those fifteen minutes, telephone business went into a slump. Theaters, as Bob Hope notes, did not open until 7:30. Later, some did open earlier. But the program was piped into the theaters so the audiences wouldn't miss a beat of the continuing saga.

Today, *Amos 'n' Andy* would be considered stereotyped and no longer acceptable. But the wonderful characters that stemmed from Gosden's and Correll's fertile minds were no minstrel-show "darkies." Both men (one of them a Southerner) had strong personal feelings about black people. So their characters, and the pickles and entanglements they got into, crossed any racial lines. These were the real roots of the program's popularity. The public readily identified with Andy's amorous entanglements, Amos's cogitations about what to name his baby daughter, and the precarious financial condition of the Fresh-Air Taxicab Company of America, "Incorpulated." (The show became a hit just about the time that the stock market collapsed.) So, on the streets and in all sorts of homes, poor, as well as affluent, people could be heard giving out Amos's high-pitched lament whenever things went wrong: "Awah, awah, awah." Or Andy's more philosophical: "I'se regusted."

In the early days of broadcasting, there was nothing comparable to the Nielsen ratings, so many shows (especially those for youngsters sponsored by cereals or soap products) began to run contests and offer prizes to gauge audience interest. For a box top or a soap wrapper, and maybe a nickel or a dime, the listener could receive a special deputy badge and secret code from the Lone Ranger,

Starting in the late 1920s, when the two gentlemen above came on the air at 7:00 P.M., virtually the whole country stopped whatever it was doing and tuned in for the latest episode of Amos 'n' Andy. Charles Correll (left) played Andy, and Freeman Gosden was Amos. The talented pair also played all the other roles on the show. "Hello, Duffy's Tavern," Ed Gardner would say as he picked up the phone in his role as the genial saloonkeeper, Duffy. Duffy's Tavern was an extremely popular show back in the good old days when beer was a nickel a glass and New York really was "Fun City." For ten years (1931–41) America went to the opera from one of the best seats in the old Metropolitan Opera House in New York City, box 44 in the grand tier (opposite), courtesy of the American Tobacco Company and NBC. There, Milton Cross (shown during an early broadcast) kept listeners abreast of the action.

Above: Jessica Dragonette, the diminutive leading soprano of the Cities Service Concerts, in 1930. Opposite top: Five big stars on the Good News Show: Franchot Tone, Robert Young, Margaret Sullavan, Frank Morgan, and Robert Taylor. The weekly show was produced by MGM and used that studio's talent exclusively. On Du Pont's Cavalcade of America: theater's "first lady," Ethel Barrymore, and actor John McIntire.

or a horseshoe-nail ring from Tom Mix, or any number of other tantalizing objects. In this way, the station and sponsor could survey the incoming postmarks and get an approximate fix on how much territory they were covering. They estimated a show's popularity by the volume of mail it received. (The ploy also became a widely used sales promotion device, making surrogate salesmen out of children who pressured their parents into buying various products so that they could get the premiums inside.)

To entertain young children, the network scheduled the *NBC Children's Hour* on Sunday mornings, starting right after the inaugural broadcast in 1926. The master of ceremonies was Milton Cross, who later became nationally known as the announcer for the Saturday afternoon broadcasts from the Metropolitan Opera House. His children's show was renamed *Coast to Coast on a Bus* and ran for sixteen years. Other kiddie shows quickly followed: *The Lady Next Door,* with child participation; *Kaltermeyer's Kindergarten,* with comedy material; *The Singing Lady,* with Ireene Wicker doing musical plays.

For farmers, there was a special Midwest show that went on the air in 1928, *The Farm and Home Hour.* It became a network weekly series in 1946.

The first women's shows were narrowly focused, to say the least: *Your Daily Menu, Your Child, Your Health, Women's Radio Review* (which was actually about current events), *Consumer Time* (in cooperation with the Department of Agriculture), *The Wife Saver, The Child Grows Up,*

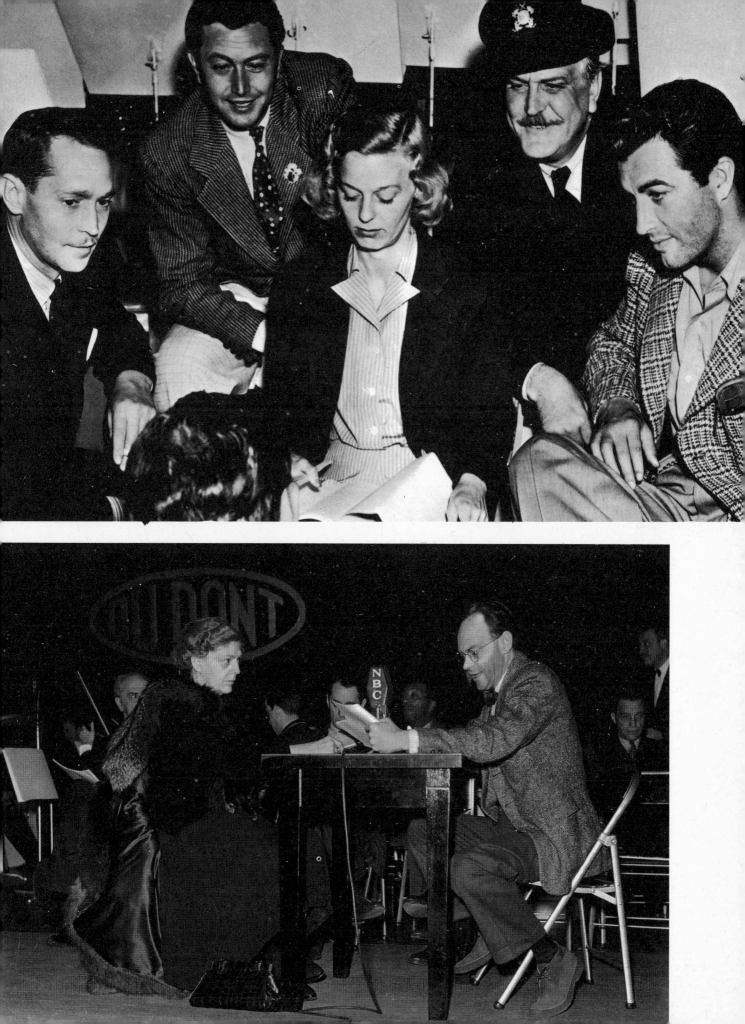

and, for wise shoppers, *Morning's Market Basket.*

Religion became a network staple, notably with *The Catholic Hour, The National Radio Pulpit* (which had the longest run, featuring prominent clergymen), *The Jewish Hour,* and *The Message of Israel.* Regularly scheduled programs were supplemented with religious specials on holidays.

TV talk and panel shows also had their origins in radio, notably the *University of Chicago Roundtable,* the *National Radio Forum* (featuring Washington political leaders), and the popular *America's Town Meeting of the Air,* which ran from 1935 to 1942.

A few years later, the Radio Guild was set up as a dramatic unit within NBC. Its name reflected New York's famous Theater Guild. In November, 1930, the Guild began a twenty-six-week series of great radio plays that was to be a network staple for the next ten years. At the same time, NBC developed a second show, *Standing Room Only,* presenting dramatizations of contemporary popular plays, and

then a third offering, *Miniature Theater,* which put on modern one-act works. Because of this, a vast rural and small-town audience discovered with delight that the theater could come to them. The effect was heightened in 1937 with the radio debut of the one great actor of whom everyone in America had at least heard: the "great profile" himself, John Barrymore. He appeared in a series called *Streamlined Shakespeare,* forty-five-minute productions including *Hamlet, Richard III, Macbeth, The Tempest, Twelfth Night,* and *The Taming of the Shrew.* Still another fine series came on the air in 1940, featuring dramatic reenactments of events that were purely American: DuPont's *Cavalcade of America.*

In no department, however, did the NBC network excel as it did in the presentation of music, both popular and classical, frequently as a public service. Band concerts in the park couldn't do much for Beethoven or Schubert. Soloists in the church were little better with Bach or Mozart. As for phonograph records, those 78s sounded pretty scratchy on the windup Victrola. Except for city dwellers, few Ameri-

The maestro himself, Arturo Toscanini (top), conducting the NBC Symphony, the finest orchestra in America at its time. Alfred Wallenstein (above) and tenor Richard Crooks in a Voice of Firestone broadcast. Air fare in 1934 (opposite) as reflected in four New York newspapers. Someone at NBC was keeping score and totalling listings per station during June.

SUBJECT *Monday*   DATE *Air*   FILE

American

LEND AN EAR TO THESE.

7:45 A. M.—Mr. and Mrs. Reader. WINS.
7:30 P. M.—Globe Trotter. N. Y. American and Hearst Metrotone News. WINS.
8:30—Gladys Swarthout. WEAF.
9:00—Rosa Ponselle. WABC.
9:30—Browning-Londos bout. WMCA.
10:00—Symphony Orchestra. WJZ.
10:30—Atty. Gen. Cumming. WEAF.
10:45—Senator Robinson. WJZ.

	DAY	mo	NBC
WEAF	2	60	⎫ 116
WJZ	2	56	⎭
WABC	1	55	
WOR	0	11	

News

MONDAY'S OUTSTANDING RADIO FEATURES

10:45 A. M.—WABC. Knights of St. John Convention.
11:00 A. M.—WEAF. U. S. Navy Band.
12:15 P. M.—WABC. Betty Barthell, songs.
1:15 P. M.—WEAF. Mayor LaGuardia and Controller McGoldrick.
1:30 P. M.—WJZ. Farm and Home Hour.
3:00 P. M.—WJZ. Radio Guild Drama—"The Shopkeeper Turns Gentleman"?
3:00 P. M.—WEAF. Rotary Convention—Mark Sullivan.
4:15 P. M.—WJZ. Pearl Curran Concert.
5:00 P. M.—WJZ. Clark's Concert Orch.
6:15 P. M.—WABC. Circus Sketch — with Uncle Bob Sherwood.
7:15 P. M.—WJZ. Mario Cozzi, baritone.
8:00 P. M.—WEAF. Sketch—"The Dog Catcher."
8:30 P. M.—WABC. Lillian Roth, Edward Nell, Ohmand Arden Orch.

8:30 P. M.—WEAF. Gladys Swarthout; Daly Orch.; Vocal Ensemble.
8:45 P. M.—WJZ. Babe Ruth.
9:00 P. M.—WABC. Rosa Ponselle; Kostelanetz Orch.
9:00 P. M.—WEAF. Horlick's Gypsies; Robert Simmons, tenor.
9:30 P. M.—WEAF. House Party.
9:30 P. M.—WABC. Gluskin Orch.; Henrietta Schumann, pianist; Three Marshalls, songs.
10:00 P. M.—WEAF. Contented Program.
10:00 P. M.—WJZ. Symphony Orch.; Sascha Jacobson, violinist.
10:30 P. M.—WEAF. Attorney-General Cummings.
11:00 P. M.—WJZ. Lombardo Orch.
11:30 P. M.—WABC. Grey Orch.
12:00 MID.—WEAF. Ralph Kirbery; Bestor Orch.

	DAY	mo	NBC
WEAF	10	202	⎫ 364
WJZ	8	162	⎭
WABC	7	151	
WOR	0	44	

TODAY ON THE RADIO

MONDAY, JUNE 25, 1934.

OUTSTANDING EVENTS ON ALL STATIONS.

10:45-11:15 A. M.—Field Memorial Mass at Convention of Knights of St. John, Syracuse—WABC.
11:00 A. M.-12:00 M.—United States Navy Band Concert—WEAF (Again on WMCA, 8:30 P. M.).
1:15-1:45 P. M.—Mayor LaGuardia and Controller McGoldrick, Speaking at Citizens' Budget Commission Luncheon, Hotel Astor WEAF.
3:00-3:30 P. M.—Mark Sullivan, Political Writer, Speaking at Rotary Convention, Detroit—WEAF.
8:30-9:00 P. M.—Gladys Swarthout, Soprano; Concert Orchestra—WEAF.
9:00-9:30 P. M.—Rosa Ponselle, Soprano; Concert Orchestra—WABC.
9:30-10:30 P. M.—World's Championship Wrestling Match, Browning vs. Londos, at Madison Square Garden Bowl—WMCA.
10:30-11:00 P. M.—Homer S. Cummings, U. S. Attorney General, Speaking at Federal Bar Association Dinner, Washington, D. C.—WEAF.
10:45-11:00 P. M.—"Legislation Compared With Platform Declarations," Senator Joseph T. Robinson of Arkansas—WJZ.
10:45-11:00 P. M.—"First Choose a Career," James W. Gerard and August Heckscher—WABC.

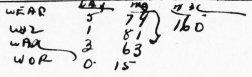

	DAY	mo	NBC
WEAF	5	79	⎫ 160
WJZ	1	81	⎭
WABC	3	63	
WOR	0	15	

Journal

Best Bets on Air Tonight

8:00—Sketch, "The Dog Catcher"—WEAF.
8:30—Gladys Swarthout, popular songs—WEAF.
9:00—Rosa Ponselle, soloist; Orchestra, Chorus—WABC.
9:00—Gypsies, Robt. Simmons, tenor—WEAF.
9:00—Minstrel Show with Gene Arnold—WJZ.
9:30—Joe Cook's House Party—WEAF.
9:30—Londos-Browning Match—WMCA.
9:30—Summer Interlude; Henrietta Schumann, pianist — WABC..

Feature Broadcasts

6:00—Baseball Scores, Clem McCarthy—WINS.
8:15—Inside Story, Edwin C. Hill—WABC.

	DAY	mo	NBC
WEAF	4	103	⎫ 189
WJZ	1	84	⎭
WABC	3	73	
WOR	0	7	

cans heard classical music or knew much about it. In a real way, NBC saved millions of Americans from musical malnutrition.

In the fall of 1928, NBC radio presented Dr. Walter Damrosch's *Music Appreciation Hour.* On Christmas Day, 1931, came *Hansel and Gretel,* the first full-length opera to be broadcast from the stage of the Metropolitan Opera House. Milton Cross, the network announcer, took his post in a private box. For the next ten years, America went to the opera with NBC every Saturday afternoon. In 1937, NBC presented its *pièce de résistance:* Maestro Arturo Toscanini and the NBC Symphony. For the next thirteen years, NBC delivered Toscanini in concert every Saturday night, frequently with noted soloists on the program.

NBC had the perfect studio for big acoustical events like Toscanini and the NBC Symphony. In 1933, Rockefeller Center was completed, and NBC became a major tenant in the towering RCA Building, which soon became universally known as "Radio City." A major feature of the new broadcast center was a mammoth studio in the middle of the building, Studio 8-H, where the Maestro and his big orchestra held forth. Over the years, 8-H has also functioned as election headquarters, an NBC Space Center for the *Apollo* flights, and has housed a variety of other major productions that require its vast and well-equipped space.

Aside from the Met and the Maestro, the network aired a spectrum of sponsored programs of both classical and semiclassical music. Noteworthy were the *Bell Telephone Hour,* the *Voice of Firestone,* and *Cities Service Concerts,* with Jessica Dragonette as leading soprano. In the popular field, there was the danceable *Lucky Strike Hit Parade,* featuring the ten top records of the week. In the era of the big bands, these included hits by Tommy Dorsey, Benny Goodman, Duke Ellington, Chick Webb, Jimmy Lunceford, and a dozen more, playing a host of tunes that are making the rounds again today.

World War II severely restricted radio. But in terms of variety of programs, the postwar period was radio's golden moment. A look at a single postwar year, 1947, indicates how much was on the air. Music occupied about 35 percent of network time that year. This included not only the NBC Symphony and Toscanini, but also other fine orchestras, the NBC String Quartet, and the Navy and Marine bands. On the lighter side, apart from the *Hit Parade,* there were half a dozen other staples, including Fred Waring and his Pennsylvanians. In the drama department, the network presented *Julius Caesar,* with Maurice Evans and Basil Rathbone; *The Magnificent Yankee,* with the Lunts; *Hamlet,* with John Gielgud, Dorothy McGuire, and Pamela Brown; and many other fine plays, including *The Late George Apley, Stage Door,* and *Our Town.* All in all, it was a classy swan song for the dear old days of radio.

Clockwise from left: A very young Gary Moore in 1941; Ozzie Nelson and Harriet Hilliard; the Maxwell House Show Boat *of the early 30s, an elaborate weekly musical review, with Charles Winninger (hat in hand) acting as emcee and captain of the showboat (he played the same role in the original Broadway production of Jerome Kern's lovely operetta, which was based on Edna Ferber's novel* Show Boat*); the pair in blackface are the vaudeville team of Malone and Padgett, known on the stage as Pic and Pat and on radio as Molasses and January; two of the topmost matinee idols ever, Carole Lombard and John Barrymore; young Richard Widmark played the title role in* Front Page Farrell, *shown here with actress Florence Williams in a photo taken at a 1942 broadcast.*

"The Art of Distant Seeing"
The Beginning of Television

As early as 1923, three years before the inaugural broadcast of NBC, David Sarnoff wrote a memorandum to the Board of Directors of RCA about something he called "television." "Television," he said, "will make it possible for those at home to see as well as hear what is going on at the broadcast station."

This idea was not as novel as one might have thought. When Marconi achieved the first transatlantic wireless transmission in 1901, engineers not only saw the implications for coding voice and music into signals that could be broadcast over great distances; they also knew that visual images could be similarly coded and transmitted. There was no great conceptual leap from transmitting voices to sending pictures. A photograph in a newspaper, as can be seen with a magnifying glass, is made up of black dots. If the dots in a particular area are densely concentrated, that area appears black. If the concentration is less intense, an area will appear gray, varying from light to dark depending on the number of black dots. It was, therefore, theoretically possible to break down a visual image into tiny electrical signals like black dots, transmit the signals, and then reconstitute the picture in a receiver. The only problem—ultimately more intractable than anyone imagined—was how to accomplish it.

"Television" was an obvious name for the coming invention. The name had well-established predecessors: telescope, telegraph, telephone. Telescope is derived from two Greek words: *tele* for "far off," and *skopein* for "to view." The derivation of telegraph is similar, coming from *graphein*, "to write." The "phone" in telephone comes from the Greek word for a sound or a voice. The word television is derived from Latin rather than Greek, originating in *visio,* the past participle of the verb *videre*, "to see." As early as 1927, Sarnoff was referring to television as "the art of distant seeing."

The earliest attempts to scan a picture or image and reduce it to a set of electronic signals were mechanical. A special camera was focused on a subject, a sitting figure, perhaps, just as in a photographer's studio. Behind the camera was a metal disc containing a row of holes punched on one radius. The disc was rotated, and as it turned, the intensity of light coming through any given hole would vary, depending on the lightness or darkness of the spot on the subject that that particular hole was "looking at." One complete rotation of the disc would, thus, provide a single image of the subject, built out of dots much like those in a newspaper photograph. To get a continuous image of a subject, particularly if it were moving, the disc was rotated rapidly. With each sweep of the disc, still pictures were produced in succession. If the subject were moving, each still reflected a change in movement. Because one image followed another so quickly, the eye registered the illusion of continuous motion. The resulting series was, then, a moving picture. The particular constellation of black and white dots generated by a single sweep of the disc could be translated into electronic impulses for transmission to a receiver elsewhere.

Aside from being cumbersome, this mechanical system presented a number of severe problems. The subject being "televised" had to be bathed with an enormous amount of artificial light. In addition, in order to reconstitute the electronic signal into an image in the receiver, the receiving set had to have a rotating disc that was identical to the one behind the studio camera. Both discs had to rotate

in precise synchronization.

As early as 1906, a completely different idea was being pursued in the laboratory of Professor Boris Rosing at the Russian Petrograd (now Leningrad) Institute of Technology. Professor Rosing believed that the solution to practical television was to be found in a new device called a cathode-ray tube, the forerunner of the modern television picture tube. Several years later, Professor Rosing convinced a promising student in electrical engineering, Vladimir Zworykin, to carry on his own interest in electronics and the future possibilities of television.

Zworykin graduated from the Institute and went off to Paris in 1912 to do graduate work in X-ray research, a related field. His studies were interrupted by World War I, after which he emigrated to America and joined the research staff of Westinghouse. There, he continued his studies in electronics, and, by 1923, he had developed a type of cathode-ray tube that was the prototype of what he later called the iconoscope. "Icono" is derived from the Greek *eikon,* meaning "figure" or "image," and the name had earlier been applied to a camera viewfinder.

The iconoscope, as ultimately perfected by Zworykin at RCA in the early thirties, provided an electronic, rather than a mechanical, key element in the television camera. Zworykin placed a photosensitive plate within a vacuum tube. This iconoscope was placed in the rear of the television camera, and the image gathered by the camera lens was projected onto the light-sensitive plate, much as the image of a conventional still camera can be projected onto a glass viewing plate at the back (or onto film located there). At the rear end of the tube was an electron gun that directed a fine

A most inauspicious beginning for television! The frightfully fuzzy image of Felix the Cat *(opposite) was produced in 1930 by the elaborate equipment above. Felix was placed on a windup turntable in RCA's labs, bathed in strong light, and rotated to give a moving object. On the table at the left is the complete transmitting equipment for NBC's experimental TV station, W2XBS.*

beam of electrons toward the plate. Other metallic elements in the gun generated an electromagnetic field, which controlled the direction of the electron beam, causing it to sweep rapidly back and forth across the light-sensitive plate, scanning the projected image line by line from top to bottom. In this way, the elements of the picture were translated into electronic impulses, which could be transmitted over a telephone wire and, later on, through the air itself via microwave relays.

David Sarnoff, another Russian immigrant, as general manager of the Radio Corporation of America, was certainly aware of Zworykin's early research at Westinghouse. So his 1922 memorandum regarding the future of television was solidly grounded. Within a few years of that date, RCA engineers were conducting television experiments of their own. Before too long, the research efforts of General Electric and Westinghouse were consolidated within RCA, as many scientists and engineers joined the RCA staff. In 1929, Zworykin himself became Director of RCA's Electronic Research Laboratory and continued developing the iconoscope there.

Two years earlier, in 1927, Bell Telephone Laboratories, part of AT&T, had experimented with a telecast between New York City and Washington, D.C., by telephone wire and cable. Another telecast was tried over the air between New York and Whippany, New Jersey. Sarnoff was delighted with the results: "With the inspiring demonstration recently made of television, the art of distant seeing, we have passed the point of conjecture. . . . Not only by wire but also by radio can an image be instantly flashed point to point. . . . The possibilities of the new art are as boundless as the imagination."

It would be a long time, however, before the technique of the art of distant seeing produced anything like artful results.

In 1928, RCA set up an experimental TV station in New York, W2XBS. By 1930, NBC took over RCA's license to operate W2XBS as an experimental television station. Ultimately, W2XBS became WNBC-TV.

In 1929, Zworykin came through with another critical invention, the kinescope. Until that time, although the prototype of an electronic iconoscopic camera had been demonstrated, the experimental receivers of the day were mechanical and the wedding of the two left a lot to be desired. The kinescope introduced the electronic principle to reception. In fact, it essentially was a mirror image of the iconoscope. Also a cathode-ray tube, it took in the signal, suitably amplified and modulated it, and then used this as input for its own

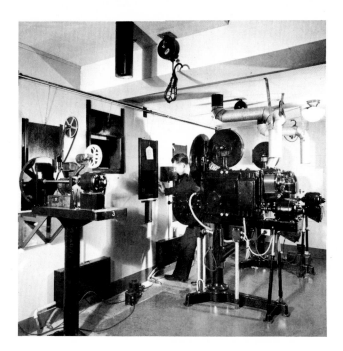

Some improvement, but no great shakes yet: a 1930s image of an ice skater on the rink at Rockefeller Plaza. In the projection booth (left) is a 35-mm movie projector. But on the other side of the wall is an early (1936) iconoscope camera that converts the movie to a television image for experimental broadcasting. A pioneer TV demonstration, a remote from Washington, D.C., featured House Speaker William Bankhead (Tallulah's father); Rep. Sam Rayburn of Texas, the Democratic leader who later succeeded Bankhead as Speaker; and Republican minority leader Joe Martin.

electron gun. The gun in the kinescope projected its beam onto a luminescent screen on the face of the tube, scanning rapidly back and forth to reproduce the same image as was picked up by the iconoscope gun. The kinescope became the first television tube, as we know it. The way was then clear to make the whole system, from camera to receiver, electronic and, therefore, capable of sustained refinement. Early images clearly indicated the need for greater precision.

To produce a satisfactory television image, the electron gun was required to sweep back and forth across the screen, as well as from top to bottom, in a fraction of a second. Otherwise, the image would not flow smoothly. With early equipment, the number of lines that could be scanned in the allotted time was limited. W2XBS went on the air experimentally with a mechanical system that could only deliver a 48-line image, which was both grainy and fuzzy. With the invention of the kinescope, the line count

rose to 60. By 1931, using a mechanical scanning camera and electronic receivers, NBC began broadcasting 120-line pictures from a transmitter atop the Empire State Building. Two years later, using the new RCA all-electronic system, the line count again doubled. By 1936, the count was 343, and it jumped again, to 441, the following year. Today, the network is full color, and the count is 525.

Paralleling the gradual improvement in picture quality was a corresponding improvement in home receivers. The earliest television sets were monstrosities that, despite their size, yielded only a small, faint, and fuzzy picture. By 1939, the picture was somewhat larger, the box somewhat smaller. But the contraption was a radiation hazard. Therefore, the image was projected vertically onto a tilted mirror, which then reflected it horizontally for the viewer. Despite the enormous technological difficulties that remained, NBC that same year inaugurated the first regular television service in the United States. Programming was spotty and lim-

NBC's first regular television service went on the air locally in 1939, and one of the features was President Roosevelt's address opening the RCA exhibition hall at the New York World's Fair. In front of the hall (above, nearing completion) is an early mobile unit. The little white car, with Freeman Gosden and Charles Correll aboard, is the Fresh-Air Taxicab. Left: A closer look at the unit. On display (opposite), an early set required a bulky cabinet to produce a rather small image.

55

ited to special events, but the few who could afford home sets were able to watch such things as President Franklin Roosevelt's address opening the RCA exhibit at the New York World's Fair, a six-day bicycle race at Madison Square Garden, the well-known actress Gertrude Lawrence in scenes from a Broadway hit called *Susan and God,* one professional baseball game, and one pro football game.

The following year, 1940, the station covered the GOP convention in Philadelphia, using thirty-four pickups from the floor tied into NBC in New York via AT&T lines. A few weeks later, film of the Democratic convention in Chicago was flown daily to New York. On election night, November 15, returns were telecast for the first time. In the spring of 1941, the Federal Communications Commission granted NBC the first commercial television license. Immediately W2XBS became WNBT, and went on the air.

The first WNBT commercial program, broadcast July 1, 1941, gave the time, the temperature, and the weather, followed by three fifteen-minute segments: a Lowell Thomas newscast, *Truth or Consequences,* and *Uncle Jim's Question Bee.* There were four sponsors: Bulova Watch, Lever Brothers, Procter & Gamble, and Sun Oil.

Little more than three weeks after FDR's unprecedented third-term election came Pearl Harbor. Few scientists or engineers were seen in the broadcast industry for another four years. When they surfaced, it was in heretofore unknown places: in Oak Ridge, Tennessee, where a massive uranium separation plant was built; in Hanford, Washington, where plutonium was produced; in Los Alamos, New Mexico, where the atomic bomb was built and tested. Some also reappeared at the Massachusetts Institute of Technology, where fundamental research in radar was conducted, and

TONIGHT THE VOICE OF FIRESTONE
AN NBC RADIO & TV PRODUCTION 8.30 TO 9PM

Visitors at the '39 World's Fair (above) check out RCA's new TV sets. An early telecast aboard an airplane (left), the durable DC-3. The nightly news was once only 15 minutes long; the anchorman was John Cameron Swayze. (It was sponsored by Camel cigarettes.) In the big Center theater at Radio City (opposite), later demolished, the Voice of Firestone went on radio and TV.

in Washington, D.C., the command post for nearly all military projects.

NBC went on the air at 9:00 A.M. on V-E Day and covered that momentous occasion for fourteen hours straight, the longest continuous telecast to that date. On V-J Day, WNBT offered nearly fifteen hours of continuous coverage.

During the mid forties, NBC began the same process with television that it had followed in the twenties with radio: building a network. In 1946, this covered a mere four cities: New York, Philadelphia, Schenectady (GE's hometown), and Washington, D.C. That same year, RCA engineers took the wraps off something very special. At their Princeton, New Jersey, laboratories they presented the first public demonstration of a new, all-electronic color television system. The color was neither very good nor very true, but it was color.

The following year, 1947, two more stations joined the fledgling NBC-TV network. About $2 million had been invested in the future of television at this point, though the revenue produced by WNBT was a mere $100,000. There were only about 14,000 television homes for the network to serve. Nevertheless, NBC went ahead, developing its programming. *Lights Out,* the popular chiller-thriller, had been brought to TV from radio the preceding year. To this were added the *Kraft Television Theater* dramatic series and, for children, the irrepressible *Howdy Doody. Meet the Press* also went on the air. The fuzzy tube offered a scheduled but unexpectedly spectacular event: the celebrated 1947 down-to-the-last-out, seven-game World Series.

If 1947 didn't look promising, 1948 proved to be quite a different story. At the beginning of the year, there were nineteen operating TV stations and 175,000 sets in American homes. By the end of that year, the industry had mushroomed to forty-seven stations with nearly a million sets sold. Television was "in." For the first time, people in their homes could see Arturo Toscanini and the NBC Symphony live, performing Beethoven's Ninth Symphony. The *Voice of Firestone* made its debut to add lighter musical fare. Audiences saw and heard Gian Carlo Menotti's two short operatic works, *The Telephone* and *The Medium,* live from Philadelphia.

Variety came in with a bang that still echoes along the corridors of NBC. Its star was a funny man named Milton Berle, on *Texaco Star Theater.* The *Philco Television Playhouse* (later the *Philco-Goodyear Playhouse*), which ultimately was responsible for such memorable works as *Marty* and *A Man Is Ten Feet Tall,* introduced plays to the TV audience. NBC News went to Washington, D.C., to look in on the House Un-American Activities Committee hearings, enabling the nation to watch with fascination the confrontation between Alger Hiss and Whittaker Chambers, masterminded by a young Congressman from California, whom many saw for the first time: Richard M. Nixon. NBC News also covered the national political conventions in expanded form with pickups from the floor and other locations. Ben Grauer and John Cameron Swayze, from NBC radio, acted as the first television anchormen, and the network gave more than forty hours of live and background coverage to each convention. For election night, Studio 8-H in Radio City was converted to election return headquarters, staying on the air until nearly midnight. It was quite a night for a TV

debut. Harry Truman, who had barnstormed the country "giving 'em hell" from the back of a Pullman car, eked out a stunning victory over his Republican rival, Governor Thomas E. Dewey of New York. Seeing as well as hearing political figures was to have a profound effect on national politics, far greater than the impact of radio alone.

Many subjects that were completely unsuitable to radio became great TV program material by the simple fact of being seen: scenic places, historical places, works of art and architecture, fashions, events great and small in nations both great and small. Feature films could now be seen in the home, and motion-picture techniques, like animation and the use of film clips, were adapted to television. The dance, magicians, acrobats, animal acts, and circuses came alive on the screen. So did drama. America followed the rise, and sometimes the fall, of Jimmy Hoffa, Billie Sol Estes, Joe McCarthy, Richard Nixon, Fidel Castro, Nikita Krushchev.

Television immeasurably enhanced the spectator value of sports, notably football and baseball. It made fads of sports that were of only marginal interest earlier: golf, tennis, wrestling, soccer, hockey.

In the late forties and early fifties, virtually all comedians defected from radio and came over to television. Since most of them were vaudeville graduates accustomed to performing before audiences, performing for the new medium came easily. Television proved to be the reincarnation of much of the dear old days of the hoofer, the clown, and the straight man.

Jackie Gleason came to TV with *The Life of Riley* (a role later taken over by William Bendix). Bob Hope's show and the *Colgate Comedy Hour* (with rotating comedians like Dean Martin and Jerry Lewis, Abbot and Costello, and Donald O'Connor) became prime-time fare.

By the close of 1950, NBC-TV had accumulated some staggering operating losses, an estimated $18 million. It was not until 1952, the twenty-fifth anniversary of the National Broadcasting Company, that the tide turned and the first profit was registered. By 1953, the number of television receivers in America reached 20 million. That same year, the Federal Communications Commission approved RCA's new system of "compatible color," which made it possible for people to receive all network programs on their old black-and-white sets, even if the program was broadcast in color. A little more than a decade later, there were an estimated 67 million TV sets across the country.

In 1956, the first videotape went on the air, providing a song sequence in color for the *Jonathan Winters Show.* In 1962, *Telstar* satellite was launched, making it possible to relay live video sequences from continent to continent almost instantaneously. In the same interval, equipment was improved and continuously miniaturized, giving news teams more and more flexibility to move about in the field. The daily network schedule was expanding in time, too. The advent of the *Today* show brought viewers early morning TV, and the *Tonight* show carried them well past midnight.

By 1965, nearly all NBC programs were in color, and the next year NBC became the first full-color network on the air. The network's capability and flexibility could at last make the possibilities of "the art of distant seeing" indeed "as boundless as the imagination."

"Only the Names Have Been Changed"

Weekly Drama

Two of the first radio classics to move to TV in the late 1940s were *Lights Out* and *Inner Sanctum.* They were quickly joined by two new shows: *Barney Blake, Police Reporter* (the first live TV drama of this type) and *The Big Story,* a weekly reenactment of an actual newspaper's crusading story break. Then, in 1952, came a trend setter: Jack Webb in *Dragnet,* which had been a popular radio show since the late 1940s. When Webb went visual, complete with his deadpan expression and low-key, clipped, matter-of-fact voice, he was an immediate success, and the show enjoyed a long run. It also gave rise to a host of trivia questions. Who played Friday's partner? (Ben Alexander) Friday's badge number? (714) The closing lines? ("The story you have just seen is true. The names were changed to protect the innocent.") The Roman numeral stamped in stone at the end of the show? (VII)

In the late sixties, NBC approached Jack Webb about reviving *Dragnet,* this time in color. Webb agreed to put his badge on once more, to return as Friday. He was joined by actor Harry Morgan, in the role of his police partner, Sergeant Frank Gannon. The revival was a huge success. The new series dealt with many problems faced by young people—LSD, alcohol, marijuana, cultism, communal living—and the programs often concluded with a sermonette delivered by Webb.

Many of the theatrical possibilities of a New York environment were mined in the late forties and early fifties. NBC introduced the *Kraft Television Theater* and then the *Philco-Goodyear Playhouse* (the sponsors alternated each week), which presented original dramas, most notably *Marty* (which later became an acclaimed feature film, with Ernest Borgnine in the title role) and *A Man Is Ten Feet Tall.* Subsequently, Alcoa Aluminum teamed with Goodyear Tire to continue presenting original dramas. Other NBC theatrical efforts of the early television years included *Studio One,* which presented *1984, Twelve Angry Men* (about a deliberating jury), and *The Dick Powell Theater,* with dramas hosted by the noted actor.

The year 1950 was notable for the debut of a first-rate series with a very long name: *Robert Montgomery Presents Your Lucky Strike Theater.* Both Montgomery and the tobacco company insisted on top billing, so they split the difference. The show specialized in hour-long adaptations of famous movies, presented on Monday nights. Among the more notable Montgomery shows was *Champion,* with a young Richard Kiley, who was later to play the *Man of La Mancha* on the stage. Other Montgomery productions included *Rebecca, The Egg and I, The Citadel,* and Thornton Wilder's *Our Town,* the staging of which included an authentic 1890s ice-cream parlor, provided NBC by the Coca-Cola Company. Even more firmly anchored in Broadway theater was *Masterpiece Playhouse,* which also began in 1950. It featured classic theater, and productions included *Hedda Gabler,* with Jessica Tandy; *The Rivals,* with that very funny lady Mary Boland; *The Importance of Being Earnest,* starring Hurd Hatfield; and *Uncle Vanya* with Boris Karloff.

By the mid fifties, drama on television was becoming increasingly innovative. *Matinee Theater* presented a one-hour dramatic show every weekday afternoon. Each drama was an original work, live and in color, and the shows featured many stars of the time (Agnes Moorehead, Richard Boone, Eddie Cantor, Geraldine Page, Vincent Price, Zsa Zsa Gabor, Hugh O'Brian, Rudy Vallee, and James Garner).

Early dramatic fare, clockwise from left: Kraft Television Theatre's 1947 production of Double Door; Patterns, also by Kraft, featured, among others, Ed Begley and Richard Kiley; Jack Webb as Sgt. Joe Friday in Dragnet, NBC's first long-running dramatic hit—the show premiered in 1952 and was revived in the late 60s; Agnes Moorehead in Greybeards and Witches, as part of NBC Matinee Theatre, which was aired during the daytime; police adventure precursor Robert Taylor's Detectives, which starred Robert Taylor and here, Tige Andrews, later of ABC's Mod Squad.

The program served as a kind of developmental workshop for perfecting techniques of color production that today are taken for granted. Because of its time slot the program could be seen on showroom sets, thus promoting NBC's push toward color TV.

A major bellwether came on the air in 1957, an hour-long show on NBC called *Wagon Train,* starring Ward Bond. By 1959, there were thirty-two Westerns on the three networks in a single season! NBC contributed to the gold rush that year with *Bonanza,* which was destined to be just that for its producers. For years it was a favorite around the world: at its peak, it was seen weekly in seventy-nine countries by an estimated 400 million people.

In 1962, NBC introduced *The Virginian,* based on writer Owen Wistar's Western classic. James Drury played the lead, supported by Lee J. Cobb. The show was the first of its kind to run ninety minutes. During that same period of the late fifties and early sixties, other thematic threads were emerging. NBC came up with a show that was to acquire the most loyal and articulate fans of almost any program in the history of television. It was, of course, *Star Trek.* The science fiction drama came on in prime time, Friday evenings, and featured William Shatner as Captain Kirk, Leonard Nimoy as Mr. Spock (with pointed ears), and the good ship *Enterprise.*

NBC scored a hit with still another type of hero in the form of a young, idealistic, and dedicated doctor named Kildare, played by Richard Chamberlain with Raymond Massey as his older colleague, Dr. Gillespie. The TV series was based on the earlier series of movies featuring Lew Ayres, who had starred in that most devastating and fearlessly honest of all World War I films, *All Quiet on the Western Front.* In the movie series, Lionel Barrymore played Dr. Gillespie, and Laraine Day played Dr. Kildare's girl friend. The television *Dr. Kildare* was destined for a long run, and proved to be the progenitor of many other doctor and hospital dramas, including such programs as ABC's *Ben Casey* and *Marcus Welby, M.D.*

The mid and late sixties were the years of the surrealistic supersleuths, sparked by the immense success of the James Bond 007 films. NBC appeared with the very popular *Man from U.N.C.L.E.,* a Bond takeoff with Robert Vaughn and David McCallum. In 1965, on NBC's *I Spy,* Bill Cosby (teamed with Robert Culp) became the first black actor to play a leading role in a series.

After the big boom in escapism, exemplified by the Westerns of the fifties and the equally escapist surrealistic capers of the sixties, the weekly drama fare on television entered a new dimension. By the 1970s the national viewing audience had become both more realistic and more sophis-

Westerns were originally made for children, who enjoyed Clayton Moore and Jay Silverheels in The Lone Ranger *(opposite), but turned "adult" in the 60s and starred the likes of Gene Barry (above) in* Bat Masterson *and Robert Fuller (left) in* Laramie.

Two immensely popular westerns were Bonanza *and* Wagon Train. Bonanza *was shown worldwide for years and starred Lorne Greene, Pernell Roberts, Michael Landon, and Dan Blocker (top).* Wagon Train *(above) opened on Wednesday nights, and it starred Robert Horton and Ward Bond and a guest star such as Ricardo Montalban. Bond played the wagon master. The acting talents of Richard Chamberlain as Dr. Kildare and Raymond Massey as Dr. Gillespie insured a long run and many imitators for the film-based television series (opposite).*

ticated, due in no small measure to a new and daring generation of filmmakers. Many a successful film appeared in movie houses that would have been considered sheer madness but a few years earlier. We had *Easy Rider, Deliverance, Little Big Man, A Clockwork Orange, The Immigrants, Midnight Cowboy, The Garden of the Finzi Continis, The Godfather, The Last Picture Show, Sounder, Bonnie and Clyde,* and *Trash,* to name but a few movies, some of which have been shown on TV.

Today's shows reflect these trends and are carefully developed in a search for authenticity and realism. Lawyers like NBC's *Petrocelli* (and, until recently, those in *The Bold Ones*) bear some semblance to real people and have clients with real problems. With the seventies came a proliferation of police and detective shows. Though all carried high entertainment and escapism values, they have often been faulted in one way or another on authenticity, both in the way they depict the police and in the manner in which they handle the law. Two assistant professors of legal studies at the University of Massachusetts did a little gumshoeing on their own, surveyed the various police and detective shows on all the networks, reported their findings in *The Wall Street Journal,* and came to this conclusion:

> . . . in the midst of all the volume of police and detective drama . . . there is one which stands head and shoulders above them all: *Police Story.* . . . It strives to present reality, and in so doing has given the American people an objective, balanced, authentic picture of the police.

In presenting just that kind of a picture, *Police Story* has apparently had quite an impact on the American public. Its subject matter is bold. The very first episode of *Police Story* concerned a black pimp and his white hustler. Still other stories involved black cops and various problems that beset black communities. The shows were so unvarnished and unbiased that they swept the top honors in the 1976 Image Awards, sponsored by the Beverly Hills-Hollywood Chapter of the NAACP. *Police Story* rates tops with cops. *The Blue Light,* a Chicago police publication, surveyed over 25,000 officers in the area and discovered that the show was the "runaway favorite of all of television's crime shows." Not only that, there has even been a sudden upsurge in applications for police work by men and women—an occupation that traditionally has trouble filling vacancies. Officials attribute this at least in part to *Police Story.* Certain episodes are now used as training films in police academies and other agencies concerned with law enforcement.

Police Story was guided on its course of authenticity by Joseph Wambaugh, a former Los Angeles police officer and writer whose works include *The New Centurions, The Blue Knight, The Onion Field,* and *The Choirboys.* Wambaugh offered story ideas from his own experience as a police officer, providing insights into the character and behavior of different types of cops confronted with specific situations. And as the show progressed, other policemen came in with ideas of their own.

The success of *Police Story* is all the more remarkable because unlike other weekly shows it has no "personality" to provide continuity. It is what is known as an "anthology series," with each episode being a self-contained story with its own cast. It is the first hour-long anthology hit in years. The show can attract top-flight actors and actresses who would prefer not to be tied down in a series. And, as in other

Westerns remained a television staple until the 70s.
Left to right: The short-lived Branded starred Chuck
Connors; the popular Virginian, which starred, among
others, James Drury, Doug McClure, and David
Hartman; two of the first—Roy Rogers and Dale Evans.

Two shows that appealed both to children and adults.
Above: Fury *starred* Fury *and featured Jim and
Joey, played by Peter Graves and Bobby Diamond.
William Fawcett also starred.* Right: Flipper *starred*
Flipper *as well as Brian Kelly, Tommy Norden, and
Luke Halpin. The show premiered in the fall of 1964.*

Preceding pages: The good ship Enterprise.
Clockwise from above: Bill Cosby and
Robert Culp as I Spy's Alexander Scott
and Kelly Robinson; Ben Gazzara as
a doomed man in Run for Your Life;
Robert Vaughn (as agent Napoleon Solo)
and David McCallum (as agent Ilya
Kuryakin) were both men from U.N.C.L.E.

Above: The Bold Ones *included lawyers, policemen, and (as shown here with John Saxon, David Hartman, and E. G. Marshall) doctors. Opposite: Dennis Weaver plays McCloud in* McCloud, *one part of the very successful series* Sunday Mystery Movie.

Clockwise from above: Peter Falk as the bemused, cigar-laden, rumple-coated Columbo; Lloyd Bridges, a television veteran, played veteran Joe Forrester, a cop; Raymond Burr, as the crippled Robert T. Ironside, is driven to work via van in San Francisco.

76

Little House on the Prairie *actually stars six people: Michael Landon, Karen Grassle (right), Melissa Sue Anderson (opposite), Melissa Gilbert, and twins Lindsay and Sidney Greenbush, who play the youngest daughter, Carrie (above).*

79

areas of television, *Police Story* has spawned its own progeny, derived from specific episodes in the parent program. The first born was *Police Woman*, starring Angie Dickinson and Earl Holliman, which was followed by *Joe Forrester*, with Lloyd Bridges.

If the success of *Police Story* demonstrated that the American public was ready for the genuine thing, the rise of NBC's unique ninety-minute *Columbo* proved something else: the public is also ready for art. *Columbo* violates practically every rule of detective drama. The murder happens at the beginning of the show, so the audience knows who did it and how and why. The hero, Detective Lieutenant Columbo (he has no first name because the creators couldn't think of one they liked), does not usually appear until the program is twenty minutes to a half-hour old. When he finally does show up, he is disheveled, disorganized, and more likely than not will start off questioning the wrong person. He bumbles about in a rumpled old raincoat (which actor Peter Falk contributed to the characterization, making it his trademark), seeming to get nowhere fast. Though he sometimes rambles on about his wife or his relatives, we never see them or his home life, or whether there are any conflicts there (which is the complete opposite of *Police Story*). He doesn't have a partner. He is a loner.

Columbo comes in from limbo and exits the same way. But wait a minute! There are elements here, "a distinct touch," as Sherlock Holmes would say. The murderer is always someone who is very sharp, sophisticated, and clever, usually an elegant member of the upper social classes, disdaining the apologetic, deferential detective. We root for the seemingly ineffectual Columbo, hoping (in vain, it appears) that he will somehow manage to finger the snobbish malefactor. This, of course, Columbo ultimately does. But he never goes out of character, even in the moment of triumph, which often comes with a casual but

Movin' On (opposite) moved off the air in 1976, but managed to make heroes of Claude Aikens and Frank Converse (who had played NYPD's Johnny Corso without cigar). Riverboat (below) featured an up-and-coming actor named Burt Reynolds. Peter Gunn was a well-constructed, offbeat detective show that starred Craig Stevens as Gunn and featured Hope Emerson as Mother (bottom). The show's class was upped by Henry Mancini, who wrote the score.

clinching afterthought: "Oh, excuse me, sir, there's just one more thing that bothers me." Whereupon the murderer knows it's all over.

It is an artfully contrived show. Columbo never uses a gun, never hits anyone, never gets hit back, never ends up in a chase. The whole appeal lies in the character of the detective and the dynamics of each situation. And in an era when an increasing number of people seem to believe that the past has nothing relevant to say to the present, the two writers and producers of *Columbo* (who also created *Mannix*), Richard Levinson and William Link, readily acknowledge Columbo's antecedents. Levinson and Link have been collaborating since college days, when they were both mystery buffs. One of their favorite characters in the classic detective literature was Petrovich, the prefect of police who behaved so deferentially toward the highly educated and intelligent murderer Raskolnikov, in Dostoevski's *Crime and Punishment.* The other character they discovered by a bit of simple detection on their own. On learning that George Bernard Shaw had a rather low opinion of G. K. Chesterton, they

reasoned that possibly Shaw was jealous of something. This led to the discovery of Chesterton's marvelous Father Brown stories, the central character of which is an eccentric, seemingly bumbling, umbrella-toting priest, who surely can be ranked as a creation in a class with Sherlock Holmes. With appropriate amendments, *voilà!* Columbo.

Columbo is not only an American success. Like a predecessor of a wholly different genre—*Bonanza*—it is an international hit as well. It is the top show in the Communist satellite countries. When Rumania ran out of *Columbos,* the national television company there flew a delegation to the United States and had Peter Falk do an ad assuring Rumanians that more shows were being made. In England, Columbo is known affectionately as "The Tatty Detective." And in Japan, where baseball is a national craze, the show accomplished the unheard-of feat of topping ball games in the ratings. It even knocked some right off the air. *Columbo* and *Police Story* are polar; yet both programs are extremely popular. It therefore appears that the future of weekly drama is wide open.

82

"Anything to Say, Dear, before the Season Starts?"

Sports

When the "Heidi affair" occurred, on the evening of November 17, 1968, the score was New York Jets 32, Oakland Raiders 29. There were only fifty seconds left to go in the game, and about 13 million pro football fans were glued to the tube for the final countdown. It was then that the game went off the air, and it was then that Oakland struck for two touchdowns, pulling off a stunning upset. The NBC switchboard in New York was completely jammed with irate calls: the efforts of NBC Sports executives in Connecticut to obtain a stay of execution, by calling the West Coast to get a direct line back to New York headquarters, came to nothing but an agonizing, frustrating zilch.

The "Heidi affair"—for all its temporary, yet monumental embarrassment—reveals a number of elements that are characteristic of NBC Sports. When game coverage failed, an enormous audience was failed. These people derive great excitement from watching "live" coverage of sports, where frequently the outcome of a game hangs in doubt until the last whistle is blown, and NBC devotes more hours to live coverage of sports than either of the other networks. A lot of that coverage is classic fare: the Rose Bowl and Orange Bowl football games back-to-back, the NCAA basketball championships, the World Series and the All-Star Game in alternating years, American Football Conference games and playoffs, and, every other year, the Super Bowl.

The first sports telecast, if it can be called that by today's standards, took place on May 17, 1939. The event was a baseball game between Columbia and Princeton at Baker Field in upper Manhattan. Princeton won in the tenth inning, 2-1. The event was televised over W2XBS, the experimental station that was later to become WNBC-TV. The television equipment was brought to the field in a big panel truck, and the truck was parked behind the bleachers. An unwieldy iconoscope camera was trained on the field, and that redoubtable sportscaster from radio days, Bill Stern, essayed to describe the proceedings. "I had no monitor," he recalled, for William Johnson of *Sports Illustrated,* shortly before his death in 1972, "and I had no idea where that damn thing was pointing." The camera's field of view was so narrow that it could not take in the pitcher's mound and home plate at the same time. Instead, it had to sweep back and forth between pitcher and batter, which was guaranteed to make viewers dizzy. Following a hit accurately was virtually impossible.

Though early television receivers cost around $600 (roughly the equivalent of $1,600 today), the screens were only five to twelve inches wide. Picture quality was poor—it looked like the game was being played in a blizzard. One reviewer said the players looked like white flies on the screen.

That same year saw a series of other television sports firsts: the first six-day bicycle race, from Madison Square Garden; the first major boxing match (Lou Nova versus Max Baer), from Yankee Stadium; the first tennis championships (the Eastern Grass Court tourney), from Rye, New York; the first professional baseball game (the Brooklyn Dodgers versus the Cincinnati Reds); and the first pro football game (Brooklyn versus Philadelphia).

World War II shut down sports programming, but after the war, equipment improved, pictures became clearer, the network expanded, and television homes proliferated. In 1947, NBC covered its first World Series. It turned out to be one of the greatest of all time: the seven-game crunch be-tween the Dodgers and Yankees that featured Al Gionfriddo's impossible catch of a sure home run off the bat of "the Yankee Clipper," Joe DiMaggio, way off against the left-field bull-pen fence. In 1951, the Series was seen coast-to-coast. By 1954, the Tournament of Roses Parade was also seen coast-to-coast—and in color. Television became a part of the environment in practically every American home, and sports grew to be one of the medium's most popular offerings.

Today, TV sports is a superbusiness that revolves around supersports and superstars. Solid sports programming has become a must for all three major networks. Bidding and competition are fierce. In 1936, the Orange Bowl Committee *paid* CBS $500 to put the game on the CBS radio network. In 1965, when NBC took over Orange Bowl telecasts, it paid the Committee $300,000 for the rights. In 1947, the Ford Motor Company and Gillette together paid out $65,000 to televise that year's entire, now-famous World Series. But in a short time, the idea of anyone sponsoring a whole Series became nothing more than a fond memory.

In 1960, CBS put up $660,000 for the rights and production costs of the Rome Olympics. But for the Munich Olympics in 1972, ABC became the top bidder with $13.5 million. ABC paid $10 million for the rights to the 1976 Innsbruck Winter Games, and reportedly $25 million for the rights to the Montreal Olympics. Rights to the 1980 Summer Olympiad in Moscow may exceed $50 million.

In the decade between 1960 and 1970, television rights to NCAA college football jumped from $3,125,000 to $12 million. The ABC 1975 NCAA football season tab was nearly $16 million, and 1976 and 1977 are anticipated to run to $18 million apiece.

From 1960 to 1970, network payments for major-league baseball climbed from $3.25 million to $16.6 million. NBC spent a reported $18 million for rights to Major League Baseball in 1975. For the next four years, rights will cost NBC and ABC together about $23 million annually.

In 1963, the combined AFL-NFL football schedule cost $7.6 million. By 1969, it was $34.7 million. Pete Rozelle, the NFL commissioner, estimates that between 1961 and 1975 the NFL collected a whopping $606 million in television rights. The three major networks paid a total of roughly $52 million for NFL rights in 1975 alone.

In 1965, the National Basketball Association received $600,000 from ABC to televise league games. In 1974, CBS paid $9 million for them.

Costs for professional golf coverage jumped from $150,000 to nearly $3 million in the decade of the sixties.

Things have come a long way from that day in 1939 when a single clumsy camera produced those first, fuzzy pictures of baseball. Typically, the networks now use half a dozen cameras, three vans filled with several million dollars' worth of electronic equipment (including a battery of monitors and two or more instant-replay machines), and deploy several dozen people for the routine coverage of one professional football game. The cost for production alone runs well over $50,000 per game. NBC and CBS cover six or seven games on a single Sunday.

To telecast a World Series game, NBC generally uses ten cameras and 60 support technicians. Covering a championship golf tournament is the real cruncher. The typical five-hole coverage requires at least a dozen cameras, several dozen microphones, eight vans filled with electronic gear, 75 to 100 people, and communications equipment to

The first sports telecast, a baseball game between Princeton and Columbia at Baker Field, May 17, 1939. The telecast was vague and hard to follow. Princeton won the game, 2–1.

link them. Mikes are buried under tees to pick up the swoosh and click as a ball is driven down the fairway. Wireless mikes are concealed on the announcers so they can move about freely, unencumbered by electronic umbilical cords. Still others are used to pick up reactions among the spectators. The last, called shotgun mikes (because they are yard-long tubes resembling shotgun barrels), are directional; they can pick up distant sounds when pointed toward the source.

Covering a major affair out on the golf links routinely costs about $300,000, but the most expensive production is, of course, the Olympics. Network bidding runs into the millions. To give one modest example: ABC spent $3 million on the 1968 Olympics from Mexico City and used forty-five cameras, 250 technicians, eight control units, and ninety-five microphones to cover the events. Both costs and coverage have risen since then. ABC is expected to spend $25 million in rights and $14 million in broadcaster's fees and transmission charges for the 1976 Montreal games.

Television can make or break a sport. In the course of a few years, TV made golf extremely popular. Result: golfers soon found it difficult to find available courses. The same thing happened to tennis when television spotted it. Result: try to get on a court today. But television nearly killed minor-league baseball. In 1939, about 15 million people attended minor-league games all over the country. By 1949, attendance was up to 42 million. Public interest in major-league teams was equally intense, but traveling to the city to actually see a game was a rare, memorable event. Instead, fans followed the home games on the radio. As the networks spread, folks could follow their favorite big-league teams

Allen "Skip" Walz (above) was the announcer for the first pro football telecast. Walz did the game live from Ebbets Field on October 22, 1939, as 13,051 fans watched the Dodgers beat the Eagles, 23–14. Ebbets Field (right) was also the site for the first televised major-league baseball game, between the Dodgers and the Reds.

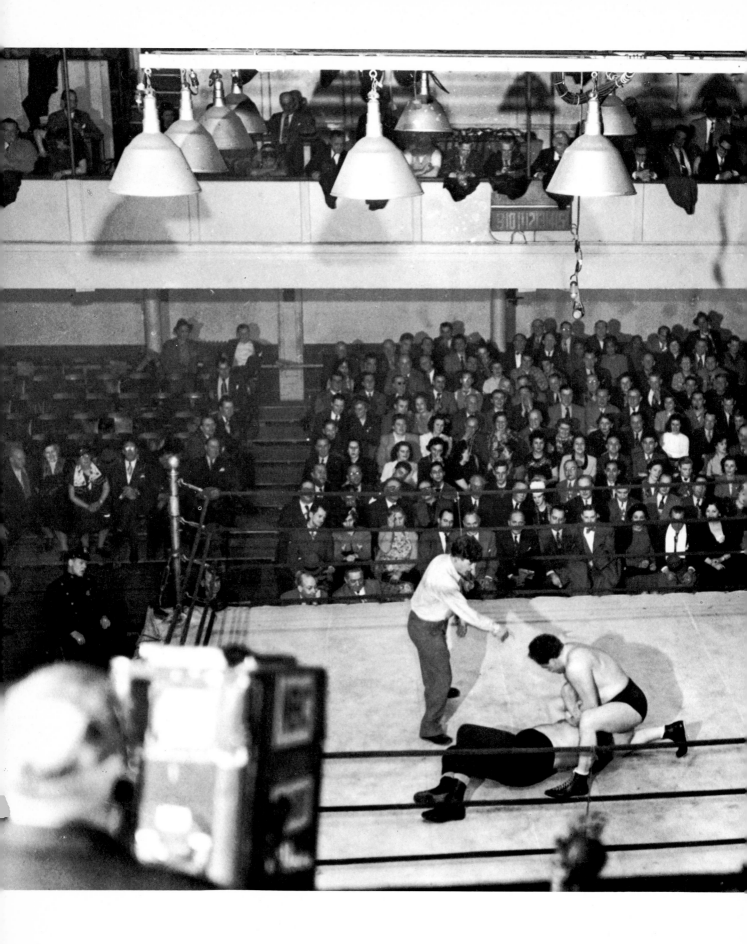

Wrestling, professional-style, was a popular staple at
St. Nick's arena in New York (left), as well as for
television viewers. And if a bar or restaurant featured
TV, they'd place it in the window for the World Series.

live, not only for home games, but on the road as well. And it was free. Naturally, interest in the minors waned.

With increasing millions of Americans watching the "national pastime" on television, the game slowly became dependent on the medium. The saga of the former Boston Braves is a perfect example. The Braves won the National League pennant in 1948 and set a season attendance record of 1,455,000. Then the management sold (for about $40,000) local television rights for most of the Braves' games for the next two seasons. By 1952, attendance had dropped a disastrous 81 percent. To salvage the team, the Boston Braves moved to Milwaukee and blacked out television coverage at their new home. The situation began to improve as the Braves gradually acquired supporters in the Midwest.

Meantime, however, the value of television air time for commercial advertising was being discovered. The cost of putting on TV commercials was escalating, bringing increasing revenues both to television and to major-league teams. This meant that baseball could be televised and still survive. It turned out that Milwaukee was a poor market because of its proximity to the larger cities of Chicago and Minneapolis. So the Braves moved again, this time to Atlanta—which offered a vast television market as yet untapped and which guaranteed the Braves $1.25 million a year for TV and radio rights.

A pattern emerged in which the success of sports and the success of television became wedded. As one television executive told Leonard Zeidenberg of *Broadcasting* magazine, "Television money is so important [to sports], if it were withdrawn, the whole structure would fall apart."

Sports people agree. Says Walter O'Malley of the Los Angeles Dodgers: "Without our national *Game of the Week* program on NBC many of our teams would be running in the red." Even the late Vince Lombardi, the fabled coach of the Green Bay Packers who was noted for his single-minded devotion to the game, agreed: "Given today's budgets, there wouldn't be a single franchise left in the National Football League without television."

These days the managers of sports go to great lengths to accommodate the managers of television. Bear Bryant, the notably successful coach of many an Alabama football team, recognizes the importance of TV: "We think TV exposure is so important to our program and so important to this university that we will schedule ourselves to fit the medium. I'll play at midnight if that's what TV wants."

In the 1967 Super Bowl in Los Angeles, the Green Bay Packers opened the second half by kicking off *twice* to the Kansas City Chiefs. NBC, which was televising the game, was in the middle of a commercial break and missed the first kickoff. Word was immediately passed to an NBC staffer on the sidelines, who notified the head referee about the error. The referee obligingly called the ball back. The second half began again, officially, so to speak. Since the networks are responsible for getting a specified number of commercials on the air during a sports event, over the years, network and football officials have worked out a system ensuring that commercial breaks will be taken only when a team calls a time-out, or after a score, or when the ball changes hands, or during the various normal time-outs that the officials call. This is to prevent unfairly breaking one team's scoring momentum.

A baseball fan who had not visited Yankee Stadium since 1947, recently took his two sons to "the house that

Early golf matches were televised by rather makeshift means, at least by today's standards (top left). The makeshift means didn't improve much when syndicated golf shows, such as Golf with Sammy Snead, made the rounds (bottom left). Shows were filmed and edited before being aired. Today's equipment (above) is about as sophisticated as can be. It includes remote cameras, roving commentators on at least five holes, and hydraulic lifts for the mobile cameras.

91

Ruth built." It was Bat Day, and the kids had been clamoring to see the real thing. Practically every time there was a close play, the father missed it. He had completely lost the habit of keeping his eyes glued to the ball and every player. He had been spoiled by television. He assumed that his kids had been spoiled, too, because they never asked to go back. Television gives the viewer the best seat in the house, now behind the plate, now behind the pitcher's mound, now zooming in for a steal of second base, or following an out-

Football coverage in the 70s is complicated and complete. Outside the stadium are three vans, one of which is known as the control unit (top). In it, at game time, are the producer, director, technical director, and assistant director. During the game, they choose the pictures, select the replays, and give instructions to the cameramen. Cameras are set up in advance (above) and checked for proper working order. They are raised to give the right sightline and are accompanied by parabolic mikes (opposite top), which catch the sounds on the field. Long-range cameras (opposite bottom) follow the general play-by-play action.

fielder chasing a fly ball. If the viewer misses a split second of action, the odds are good that he will be shown the close one, and from the best angle. He will probably see the whole thing slowed down, too, perhaps frame by frame. The whole experience is truly a remarkable electronic feat.

A look at how NBC covers an NFL game—an ordinary game, not a big playoff or the Super Bowl (where even more equipment is brought in)—is as good a study as any for the anatomy of electronic sports.

Planning begins many months in advance. As the game is scheduled, air time is allotted, circuits and equipment are committed. An NBC crew is assigned to the game: a producer, director, their assistants, a technical crew, and the two commentators who will describe the progress of the game from the broadcast booth. The announcers are supported by a spotter for each team who knows all the players and their numbers by sight. There is also a runner who scuttles back and forth between the broadcast booth and a second nearby booth occupied by a number of statisticians. These statisticians furnish vital figures as the game progresses: yardages gained, passes completed, number of turnovers, team rankings, statistics on individual players' accomplishments. The data given by commentators are not casually obtained.

Thursday and Friday before any Sunday NFL game find the producer, the director, and the two commentators making preparations. NBC's top announcers, Curt Gowdy and Al De Rogatis, are well matched. Gowdy is a veteran sportscaster, who largely covers the play-by-play description of the game. De Rogatis, a retired pro ballplayer himself, offers analytical comments from his experience and does what are called color pieces. He describes a particular player's achievements, a coach's record, a team's adeptness at sacking the opposing quarterback, for instance, or putting on a blitz.

The Thursday and Friday "prep" sessions are devoted to scouting the two teams that will be playing on Sunday. Who's hot, and who's not? Who's injured and out and who's hurting but may play? What will the game strategies be? The sportscasting team knows many of the players personally and can phone them for information. The public relations men for the teams, and even the coaches themselves, provide additional input to the network research efforts. Psyching out the two teams in depth and in advance requires considerable confidence between the sports team and the athletic teams, because while researching, NBC may well learn something about one team that the opposing team would like to know.

The broadcast team must be up, alert, anticipating the next play before it occurs, if possible, working smoothly in a coordinated effort, just like the players on the field. Everyone knows that if an event is missed (an interception where a defending back comes out of nowhere, or a stealthily concealed pass to the outside), it is gone forever. As far as the viewing public is concerned, if it was not on camera, it never happened. The cameramen, too, are veterans; they rely to some extent on instinct for knowing where and how to follow the action.

On Saturday, the sports team sets up in the stadium and city that will host the game. The producer, director, and commentators decide which running backs to follow, which linebackers to focus on. A notable "headhunter" is always a likely prospect. They discuss what to say in the brief pregame show, which should be concerned with a topic that

may be critical to the outcome of this specific game—the condition of a star quarterback, or the strength of a particular defensive unit. If possible, they observe the teams at practice.

Three large vans, or mobile television units, are parked outside the stadium gates. One is for storage. Another houses the video technicians, tape editors, and sound men. For an average game, the technical unit includes two engineers, each of whom is in charge of an instant-replay unit. Each replay unit can record the output of only one of the cameras on the field. It is up to the director to make an on-the-spot decision about which field camera may be a likely candidate for instant replay. The replay unit records the output of the camera it is connected with on videotape. This is quickly rewound for showing. Another type of replay unit—for slow motion—records the image on a metal disc.

The third van is the control unit. At one end is an array of twelve television monitors (as many as eighteen would be there for the World Series or the Super Bowl because more cameras would be on the field). Six of them record what is being picked up by the six cameras used for the game. Four of these cameras are in the stands. One is at each twenty-five-yard line to pick up the game as it moves downfield in either direction. One is at a far end of the field to provide an overview as well as close-ups of goal-line activity and extra points. (The twenty-five-yard-line camera covers this at the other end of the field.) A fourth camera is directly above the fifty-yard line, in the broadcast booth. This camera can take in a broad view of the field, zoom in for tight-action shots at midfield, and turn to pick up the "talent" in the broadcast booth for their frequent live appearances during the game. The fifth camera is down on the sidelines, mounted on a mobile platform that can be driven from one end of the field to the other, following the tide of the game as it surges back and forth. All these cameras are essential to keep the viewer's chair moving so he can get the best possible look at the action. The sixth camera is a portable affair, known to the crew as a "creepie," with which a cameraman can move freely about the field, taking in action on the players' benches or observing coaches or injured players. The creepie is also used for interviewing officials and celebrities in the stands.

The other six monitors handle the commericals, any film or videotape inserts (highlights of previous games), the SloMo (short for slow-motion) replays, and, frequently, a seventh, isolated camera covering one particular player.

The director briefs his cameramen, but once the game starts, the cameramen will be pretty much on their own because the director cannot simultaneously talk to one or another of them and switch from one camera to another at the control console in the main van. However, all the cameramen wear headsets so they can listen in on what the announcers are saying from the broadcast booth high up over the fifty-yard line. This guides them as they follow the action. Moreover, all the members of the sports team are interconnected by a closed-circuit voice system, so they can all communicate if need be. The director constantly calls the cameramen's attention to important aspects of the game. Nevertheless, these men are experienced at covering football and generally know how to follow the game without direction. They know how to contend with the difficulties and subtleties of play, too. A cameraman who knows football will watch the defensive lineman. Sometimes it is easy to lose a punt high in the air, against the background of the crowd. Here the cameraman has other resources: "I usually look over the top of the camera and try to move to the receivers downfield," explains one.

As game time approaches, the talent assembles in the broadcast booth for the pregame show. Aside from the spotters and runners, the booth holds another member of the NBC crew: a stage manager who makes sure operations go smoothly. Both announcers have a book containing material they will read during the course of the game (background bits, commercial lead-ins, promotional blurbs, and the like). A second stage manager is stationed on the sidelines to tell the officials when NBC is using a time-out for a commercial.

The director sits at the center of the console in the control van with the producer to his left and the technical director to his right. Nearby is a fourth member of the team, the associate director. The director, eyeing the field camera monitors, will switch from one to another to produce the actual coverage of the game. He is responsible for what the TV audience actually sees. The producer is responsible for supervising the overall coverage of the game. Once the game is underway, the producer decides when to use replays, when to ask for commercials, and when to insert visuals. The technical director mans the master control board, which connects all the cameras, sound equipment, video machines, and transmission equipment. The associate director handles what remains, which amounts to quite a bit. His headset connects him to the visuals room, and when he anticipates the need to display a score or some other set of statistics, he will call for it. When it appears, on a separate visuals monitor, he knows it is available to go on the air. He is also connected to the stage manager in the announcing booth so that he can alert the commentators as the time approaches for them to provide a promotion or lead-in to an upcoming commercial. He has still a third line to the fieldside stage manager, for coordinating time-outs with the officials.

The whistle blows. The game begins, and so does the parallel contest in the control van. The director stares at the monitors of the six field cameras and begins calling out, "Take one. Take four. Take two," meaning switch in camera one, then cut to camera four, then to two. As he calls out the numbers, the technical director punches the appropriate buttons on the control console, which in turn send the visual from each camera out over the air. Everything rolls with a kind of tense rhythm as the director feels out the game in progress, focusing on the quarterback as he calls the signals, cutting to another camera as the quarterback drops back in the pocket to pass, then to a camera showing a long view for the throw, then to another camera that is concentrating on an end racing downfield as he gathers in the ball. The producer calls for the replay units to roll, and the replay is shown. The whole production is interspersed with commercial breaks, takes with announcers, and sideline color. It is a fabulous human and technological achievement.

"Good Night, David"

News and Special Events

At 1:34 P.M. (12:34 Central Time) on Friday, November 22, 1963, a message registered on the United Press International teletype in the NBC newsroom:

DALLAS, NOV. 22 (UPI). THREE SHOTS WERE FIRED AT PRESIDENT KENNEDY'S MOTORCADE IN DOWNTOWN DALLAS.

It was from Merriman Smith, the UPI senior White House correspondent covering John F. Kennedy's trip to Fort Worth and Dallas. A few minutes later, a dispatch came over the AP ticket from Jack Bell, the Associated Press man at the scene. It had been hopelessly garbled by a grief-stricken operator:

DALLAS, NOV. 22 (AP). BLOOD STAINEZAAC REMTHING, HE LAAAAAAAAAAAA.

Stanley Rotkewicz, the production manager was alone in the offices of *The Huntley-Brinkley Report* (now *NBC Nightly News*) when the messages came in. He looked idly at the UPI ticker as it began its characteristic clack-clack-clack-clack. But then, as he recalls, "When I saw the message, I practically ripped the whole damn machine right off

the wall!" Rotkewicz was among the first at NBC to learn of the tragedy. It became his job to pass the word, setting off a top-speed effort to rally NBC personnel across the nation.

At 1:36, ABC radio's Don Gardiner interrupted local television programming with Merriman Smith's first message. At 1:40, CBS cut in on *As the World Turns*. Walter Cronkite announced: "In Dallas, Texas, three shots were fired at President Kennedy's motorcade. The first reports say that the President was 'seriously wounded.'"

Another five minutes passed before NBC put the news on the air. One reason for the delay was its reliance on the Associated Press. In many journalistic establishments, the

The events surrounding President Kennedy's assassination were televised for over 71 hours. NBC employed more than 400 newsmen and technicians and 33 mobile units. The tragic weekend was carried worldwide by satellite.

AP had long been considered the more reliable and conservative of the two wire services. NBC wanted confirmation from the AP. Unfortunately, that service was having its own troubles in those early minutes, and Jack Bell was having difficulties getting a reliable connection with his Dallas office. Compounding the problem was the fact that at that point the NBC television network was "down"—it was in one of the periods of the day when affiliated stations were originating their own programming.

In New York, WNBC-TV, the local station there, was running *Bachelor Father*. At 1:45, the program was interrupted for an NBC News Bulletin voice-over announcement:

President Kennedy was shot at in Dallas, Texas, today. Blood was seen on the President's head as they rushed him to the hospital. Mrs. Kennedy was heard to exclaim, 'Oh, no.'

Less than two minutes later, a second NBC News Bulletin went out:

President Kennedy and Governor John Connally of Texas were cut down by an assassin's bullet in downtown Dallas and were rushed to an emergency room at Parkland Hospital. The President's limp body was seen cradled in the arms of his wife. There is no information at present on his condition.

About six and a half minutes after that, at 1:53:12 P.M., all regular network programs were cancelled. Bill Ryan and Chet Huntley went on the air live. News from Dallas was sketchy at best, but they made do with what they had. At 2:05 P.M., Frank McGee talked on the phone to NBC Newsman Robert MacNeil, who had been covering the presidential trip and was then at Parkland Hospital. McGee went on the air to add a few more details provided by MacNeil. At

2:15, a brief report came in live from Charles Murphy of NBC's Fort Worth affiliate, WBAP-TV. At 2:19, David Brinkley reported from Washington, D.C., that Congress had recessed and that Congressmen were now watching NBC to see what was happening. Senator Edward Kennedy, Brinkley reported, had been informed by Senator Mike Mansfield of the shooting of his brother.

The newsmen who anchored those early broadcasts all knew the President, some of them quite well. And it was difficult for them to maintain a dispassionate attitude on the air. William Manchester, in *The Death of a President*, reported that David Brinkley, when he came on, was in a state of what another NBC newscaster described as "controlled panic," and his composure vanished when he was off camera. Bill Ryan and Frank McGee were in tears when they were finally relieved. It was Ryan who had reported (shortly after 2:30) on the network that the President was dead.

Gradually, the media got themselves together, and the nation—soon much of the world as well—began watching an American tragedy unfold. More and more NBC newsmen checked in from the bureaus, from affiliates, from posts at the United Nations, and from foreign countries. In a very short time, nearly all the incredible resources of the American communications industry were focused on Dallas. During the early hours, the nation was ripe for panic: it was easy to believe the assassination of President Kennedy was the result of a secret conspiracy, perhaps international in scope. By mid afternoon, Tass, the Soviet news agency, announced, with no justification whatever, that the assassin was "a man of the extreme right-wing element."

Aboard *Air Force One*, Lyndon Johnson was well aware of the national uncertainty. He had himself sworn in as quickly as possible, then took off for Washington. The first thing he did on landing at Andrews Air Force Base was to appear on television, assuring the nation that presidential

Although the means were more crude years ago, the intent was similar. Clockwise from top left: AP and UPI teletypes bring the news; John McVane reports from the U.S.S. Missouri; *gubernatorial results are chalked in.*

continuity had been effectively maintained.

Coverage of the assassination of President John Kennedy—and the events of the following days, which included the state funeral—was what is known as an "instant" news special. This type of news coverage can preempt the network, taking the place of regular programming, at any time, for any fast-breaking story that NBC News considers of national importance. The assassination of the president was far and away the most important special of the television era, for NBC and the other networks as well. It has been estimated that out-of-pocket expenses incurred by the three networks in covering those events, in addition to loss of revenues from cancelled commercials, totaled $9 million. NBC devoted 71 hours, 36 minutes to reporting, on that long and fateful four-day weekend. More than 400 newsmen and technicians went into action at key points across the country. Thirty-three mobile units, with one to six cameras each, were part of the operation. Scenes of President Kennedy's funeral were relayed to Europe via satellite, and European reactions were relayed to the United States by the return route. These satellite relays made it possible for twenty-three countries, with a combined population of more than 600 million people, to witness these events.

In 1975, NBC News presented a total of 1,960 hours of radio and television programming. Over 720 hours of regularly scheduled TV hard news were presented. In addition, there were 91 hours of special programming. NBC pro-

cessed 18 million feet of color news film, enough to reach from coast to coast, and more than all the film used in all the Hollywood and New York feature productions that year.

Ordinarily, news specials take months to prepare and are usually aired with commercial sponsorship. Special news events of this type are political primaries, national conventions, and election-night returns. NBC's skills of reporting national conventions were firmly established in 1956, during the Democratic convention in Chicago. That was the year that Chet Huntley and David Brinkley first teamed to offer their pungent observations and clear analyses of the hoopla and confusion. Eight years later, at the Republican National Convention in the Cow Palace near San Francisco (which overwhelmingly nominated Barry Goldwater, who in turn was buried by the LBJ landslide), Brinkley was asked to explain this uniquely American show to bewildered Europeans watching it via satellite. His now-classic explanation: "It is partly political, partly emotional, partly propaganda, partly a social mechanism, partly a carnival, and partly mass hysteria. It can be described as nonsense, and it often is—but somehow it works."

Showing people just how conventions work represents a technological achievement in its own right. In the early days of radio, a handful of people, in a room with a few telephones and typewriters, did the trick, in audio only. In the early days of television, a dozen or so reporters on the floor, in touch more or less with the control booth above them, handled both the audio and the visual.

The ability actually to witness political spectaculars, something that we take for granted today, began very modestly. Before the advent of radio, people read about conventions in newspapers. Though the accounts were obviously after the fact, there was, nevertheless, excitement generated by "extras," announcing the unexpected. The first radio coverage of a convention was in 1924. AT&T's pioneer New York City station WEAF (later the key station of NBC) arranged a special twelve-station, coast-to-coast network using telephone lines to cover the Republican convention in Cleveland. (Subsequently, similar coverage picked up the Democrats. in New York.) Graham McNamee, a young sportscaster, was assigned to the conventions and became, in effect, the first anchorman. An estimated 3 million Americans listened on earphones or gathered around loudspeakers as the Republicans nominated Calvin Coolidge.

Over the years, both technology and coverage improved. By 1928, the new NBC network was on the air with forty-eight stations, and Graham McNamee was its top announcer. In 1932, with eighty-eight stations, NBC introduced parabolic microphones, five to six feet in diameter, which were directional and could pick up sounds at great distances. One of them accidentally zeroed in on a scraping chair, amplified the sound, and transmitted it as a great roar over the public-address system. It sounded as though a balcony were collapsing and created a momentary panic.

Television coverage debuted in 1940, picking up the Republicans in Philadelphia and telecasting the convention in New York over NBC's experimental station, W2XBS. That year, a mere handful of people, an estimated 50,000, actually saw Wendell Willkie nominated. After World War II, however, the television networks expanded rapidly and convention coverage improved markedly. Videotape was introduced in 1960, making it possible to record several events simultaneously and air them at will. As in football, videotape made possible the instant replay. By 1964, the network was sending sixty tons of equipment to San Francisco to cover the Republicans, then moving it all back to Atlantic City for the Democrats. That year, NBC News used fifty cameras and built four complete broadcast control facilities in each city.

Around NBC, the most memorable event of the conventions was an unexpected one. In San Francisco, in one of their periodic, always futile, clearings of the aisles, Republican officials ejected John Chancellor, then a floor reporter, from the scene, while he continued to report in full view of the TV camera. Just after he disappeared from the camera's range, he signed off with: "This is John Chancellor, NBC News, somewhere in custody."

In the early days of television, NBC News was something of an orphan, even though some very competent reporters and writers, producers and cameramen, were involved in preparing it. The evening news, with John Cameron Swayze, was a mere fifteen minutes long. News specials were a rarity. With expanding convention coverage by NBC News, however, this situation began to change.

In 1972, both the Republican and Democratic conventions were held in Miami. The way NBC News organized *Decision '72* set a pattern in sophisticated electronic journalism. Planning for *Decision '72* began immediately following the 1968 conventions, with changes being made as technological developments occurred, particularly in the area of miniaturized equipment. As convention time approached, NBC News descended on the Miami area with

Above: Soon after Chet Huntley and David Brinkley joined Bill Henry for the 1956 Republican convention, the pair was chosen to anchor the evening news. Top: 1968 Republican convention. Left: Control unit, 1972, at Miami Beach.

101

thirty-five trailers of various sizes loaded with television equipment, including a number of multi-ton mobile units that came from as far away as Los Angeles. The news staff assigned to television and radio coverage added up to about 450 people, including reporters, editors, writers, and technicians. In addition, about one hundred temporary workers provided supplementary services: secretaries, messengers, copy boys, security men, and porters.

At the Miami Beach Convention Hall, a complex of several dozen trailers and additional mobile units was set up. The array of vans within the hall contained radio studios, a complete TV transmitting station, newsrooms, three mobile units connected to cameras within the hall, videotape facilities, a command deck with a complete master TV control system for directing convention coverage and determining what went on the air, and when, and executive offices. The ancillary vans outside the hall housed support facilities: engineering units, film-processing labs, a film-editing complex, Press Department facilities, a first-aid station, and production quarters for *NBC Nightly News*. During the conventions, the other regular news programs originated in Miami as well, including the *Nightly News*, with John Chancellor and David Brinkley; *Meet the Press*, hosted by Lawrence Spivak; and *Today*, with Barbara Walters and Frank McGee.

To provide full-color coverage within the convention hall, eleven cable-connected cameras, capable of operating in poor lighting conditions, were located strategically around the arena, supplemented by the single portable TV camera that was permitted on the convention floor. A thirteenth camera was stationed outside the main entrance.

NBC News was not only at the convention, it was all over the Miami area. There were "plug-in" remote installations at the hotels housing both the Democratic and Republican party headquarters as well as at the half a dozen other hotels that housed candidates and state delegations. Four mobile units were on the alert around the clock to move quickly to any of these locations should an important development occur. In addition to the mobile units, NBC had eleven film crews and thirteen reporters on hand, to cover the arrival of politicians at Miami Airport, activities at hotels, press conferences, public meetings, and demonstrations. All this outside activity was coordinated from the smallest room in the electronic complex of the Broadcast Center at the Convention Hall, a four-by-five-foot cubicle that housed the assignment editor. It was all the space he needed to juggle his field units efficiently.

For this phase of *Decision '72,* NBC had four reporters on the floor of the convention hall—Douglas Kiker, Catherine (Cassie) Mackin, Tom Pettit, and Garrick Utley. Just off the floor was Edwin Newman, a former floorman himself, who interviewed candidates, party leaders, and other politicians, on special assignment. A far greater number of reporters was working the environs. Individuals were assigned on a one-to-one basis to each of the major candidates, as well as to groups like the National Committee, the Black Caucus, youth groups, and areas like the podium itself and the periphery of the convention floor. Still others—such as Tom Brokaw and Bob Teague—were available for general assignments as they came up. An additional twenty-one reporters covered twenty-nine of the most important state delegations.

Overseeing the whole drama were NBC's two anchormen for the conventions, John Chancellor and David Brinkley, perched high above the floor in a glass booth twenty-five feet wide and eight feet high. Viewers of previous conventions had written to NBC expressing some concern that this highly visible pair never seemed to get anything to eat, despite the fact that their vigil lasted a dozen hours each day. The network had put out a news release assuring people that during confinement, Chancellor and Brinkley would receive catered meals. After it was all over, however, Chancellor commented: "The trick to staying awake and alert during those long sessions, I think, is not to eat a lot." His cell mate concurred. "I eat less," said David Brinkley, "for lack of time to eat."

Decision '72 worked very well for NBC. The network delivered a quality product to the American electorate, and the electorate responded in kind by delivering to NBC by far the best ratings (an estimated 115 million viewers watched *Decision '72*). The production cost NBC several million dollars, the price of an unextravagant feature film. NBC tabulated an eclectic list of what just a few of the expenditures had been:

—1 boat on standby to take key personnel to the Convention Center in case of a traffic tie-up
—six orthopedic beds for anchormen and producers
—1 gasoline generator in case of a power failure
—7,000 gallons of bottled water
—5 binoculars to spot celebrities on the floor
—250 cars
—50 bottles of suntan lotion plus 1,500 salt tablets for those working outdoors
—125 cans of bug spray
—1,000 telephones
—20 refrigerators
—50 special "beeper" paging devices
—1 birthday cake for John Chancellor

Another special event that drew increasing coverage over the years, developing its own technological revolution, was the space race. In 1956, the Air Force was firing rockets from Cape Canaveral, Florida. It was furtive about its schedules. Jim Kitchell, general manager of NBC News Services (responsible for physical facilities and photographic equipment), was covering the Cape and compiled a Who's Who of people involved in launch activities. Then, by asking who was in town any particular week or day, he could determine whether or not something was going to happen. The larger the gathering of names, the greater the likelihood of a launch. But when?

The Air Force had a tall pole in its compound. At appropriate times, a red ball was run up to the top. This was a signal to the offshore fishing fleet to clear the area, indicating a launch was close at hand. But what day? At what time? By casually asking the motel manager when people were leaving breakfast calls for the next day, Kitchell pinpointed launch times quite precisely. His crew filmed these launchings from the beach. The early results were of poor quality because distances were great, missiles were not as spectacular as they later became, and tracking them with standard camera equipment was a problem.

On October 5, 1957, the Soviets launched into orbit *Sputnik* (the Russian word for fellow traveler). A few years later, on April 12, 1961, their first cosmonaut, Yuri Gagarin, was up. Shortly after *Sputnik*, the Air Force fired its first Vanguard rocket from the Cape, and NBC News covered the event live via radio-telephone (without pictures). Subse-

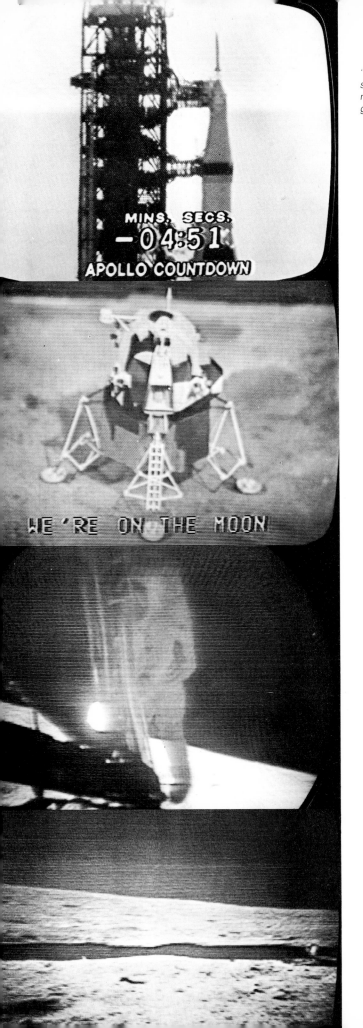

"The biggest show in broadcast history" as seen from the screen, top to bottom: Apollo XI *countdown; touchdown on the moon; Neil Armstrong's "one small step for a man, one giant step for mankind"; the moon's surface, a kind of desert.*

103

Above: Versatile mobile unit prepares for the telecast of the 1971 White House wedding. Top: For the first time in history, live pictures of China are sent back to the U.S.

quently, Kitchell rented a house on the beach and had a camera platform constructed for better filming. Suspicious neighbors reported these activities to the police.

Kitchell kept pressing to film a shot live from the Cape itself. In the summer of 1958, officials finally relented and said NBC could shoot a launch but could not go on the air until there was "fire in the tail"—meaning the ignition and launch had to be a successful one. (There were frequent troubles with these early firings, and the Air Force did not want to make its first public airing with an abort.)

Starting with the Gemini Program, pairs of astronauts began orbiting the earth. *Apollo IX* made the first trip to the moon, but the extravaganza was the flight of *Apollo XI* in 1969, which culminated in Neil Armstrong and Ed Aldrin piloting their LEM, the *Eagle,* to a soft landing on the lunar surface (a touch-and-go affair for a few moments, with Armstrong taking over the manual controls). To cap the climax came Armstrong's message as he became the first man to set foot on the moon: "That's one small step for a man; one giant step for mankind." According to the A.C. Nielsen Company, the lunar landing drew the largest United States audience ever attracted by a single event—125 million viewers who individually logged an average of fifteen hours watching TV. (A higher percentage of homes had tuned in to President Kennedy's funeral six years earlier, but there were fewer TV sets in existence then.)

NBC devoted sixty hours to the lunar flight, thirty-two of them to the actual landing, and won an Emmy Award for its coverage. Commented *Broadcasting* magazine, "It took a minimum of $11 million in expenditures and in revenue loss, and an estimated 1,000 personnel for the networks to produce what had to be the biggest show in broadcast history."

While tracking the Gemini and Apollo Programs, all three networks vastly improved both their camera work and backup graphics. Television cameras followed the rising rockets with ever-improving steadiness, close-up detail, and for longer periods: a far cry from the early, distant, wobbly, and fleeting glimpses televised at the beginning of the space program. NASA made highly sophisticated tracking devices available to television cameras and included on-board cameras for in-flight coverage. It was good public relations. NASA was well aware of the program's cost to the public. John Kennedy, speaking in Houston the evening before he was assassinated, made a verbal slip in this regard. He announced that in a month the United States would launch the biggest booster rocket to date, firing "the largest payroll—payload—into space, giving us the lead" (in the space race). He added, "It *will* be the biggest payroll, too."

The most impressive sight from the space program was the view back of a small, beautifully colored, and fragile planet suspended in the black void of lifeless space— spaceship earth, the home of mankind. Seeing the earth as it actually is, a solitary but life-supporting planet, had implications for ecology and human psychology, providing a sense of unity on earth that will linger in our collective consciousness. It will be hard to rate any future special as covering a more significant event than the flight of *Apollo XI.*

The drama begins to unfold casually around ten o'clock each weekday morning. The stage is an open room approximately fifty feet by fifty feet. In the early hours, the room seems large and empty. Only a few members of the *Nightly*

Top: Meeting in executive director Les Crystal's office, where decisions will be made about what goes on the Nightly News. Above: The newsroom, which includes six television monitors to assess the competition, a cluster of desks, and an extensive telephone system.

105

News team are on hand. There are about fifteen desks in the room, most of them arranged along walls or beside an occasional piece of communications equipment. Half a dozen of the desks are pushed together in an apparently haphazard way near the front of the room. The arrangement is actually quite deliberate. It is the classic formation that makes up the city desk of a metropolitan newspaper, making possible efficient communication among the people who supervise a big news operation. The wall decorations are bulletin boards with lists of assignments, postcards from friends, cartoons, and an occasional joke or quote ("Aetsa not *my* chobb, man!"—made famous by Freddie Prinze of *Chico and the Man*).

In the big room, on shelves, is a collection of reference books: dictionaries, gazetteers, atlases, volumes of facts and statistics. There are also two DEX machines, similar to wirephoto and copying equipment. Each machine contains a rotating cylinder around which is wrapped a sheet of photosensitive paper that receives incoming graphics. The connection is made to a transmitting DEX machine by telephone. When a drawing, photograph, or text is to be transmitted, the sender calls the destination and indicates which line will be used. Transmission time averages two minutes per page. NBC leases several such telecopiers, located in Washington, D.C.; Chicago; Burbank, California; and London. A portable DEX is used routinely for on-site coverage of national conventions.

Aside from the telecopiers, the newsroom has all three wire services, UPI, the AP, and Reuters, which feed copy to NBC continuously via teletype, as they do to the newspapers and other journalistic centers around the world that subscribe to their services. Along opposite walls of the room there are two identical sets of TV monitors, arranged so that at least one set is visible from almost any point in the newsroom. Among other things, these enable the *Nightly News* crew to watch the evening news programs on the other two networks so they can assess their competition.

Off the main room are a number of offices. One is for anchorman John Chancellor, one is for Les Crystal, the executive producer of the *Nightly News*. A third houses a unit that produces a new regular feature of the program entitled *Special*—in-depth explorations of matters of serious national concern. This new unit has its own producer and a staff of three people. It can call on NBC newsmen anywhere in the world for assistance in its investigations. Since a solid piece of investigative reporting requires substantial air time to present, these stories are broken down into segments and aired on successive evenings. The creation of this unit adds a new and important dimension to the *Nightly News*.

Two floors above the newsroom is the graphics department, which produces artwork for various news groups, including the *Nightly News*. Here, artists generate most of the graphics that are projected onto the screens behind Chancellor to illustrate news events. Since news events generally involve specific areas, and technical atlas-type maps would not provide good visual material for television, the graphics department prepares its own maps to highlight the exact locations of events. Such maps might show the area of a border dispute in the Middle East, or the site of an oil spill in the Chesapeake Bay, or an area in eastern Arkansas that has been flooded by the Mississippi River.

The graphics department also makes use of an extensive photographic file. A picture of the Eiffel Tower makes an identifiable background for a news story from Paris; a view of a huge oil refinery is appropriate for the latest item about the energy crunch. The group also maintains a photo file of people in the news, assigns photographers when needed, or commissions artists to produce color portraits.

By ten in the morning, Stanley Rotkewicz, the production manager, has been on the scene for at least an hour. His myriad responsibilities include all of the equipment in the big room, so he arrives early to check the DEX machines, the teletypes, and the monitors. Then the others stroll in. John Chancellor goes to his office, takes off his jacket, and then heads for a small desk and typewriter by the front windows overlooking New York's Forty-ninth Street. Except for an occasional trip to his office to make a personal phone call, to receive a visitor, or to pick up another pipe and tobacco, this will be his station for the rest of the day. At about 6:15 P.M., he puts his jacket on, straightens his necktie, and heads for Studio 3-K to go on the air with the *Nightly News*.

The cluster of desks nearby is used by Harry Griggs, who acts as national news editor; Edward Fouhy, the producer, who reads and initials all copy before it goes on the air; and Gilbert Millstein, the principal writer and copy editor. Nearby is the door to Les Crystal's office, which is generally open. Along one wall of the office is another set of television monitors, and on Crystal's desk is a small telephone switchboard capable of handling conference calls among the NBC News Bureaus. It is the largest office and serves as a conference room for discussions that may involve as many as a dozen people. As executive producer, Crystal is responsible for tracking all items that are candidates for a particular evening's news telecast: those that are in and already edited, those that are expected (he must know the source of the item and its schedule), those that are due as satellite relays, and those that will potentially be late-breaking headlines.

The network news team's credentials are solid. Millstein was a reporter with *The New York Times* for thirteen years before coming to NBC in 1965. Griggs started as an NBC reporter, then went to CBS, and subsequently returned to his alma mater. Before he joined the *Nightly News*, Ed Fouhy was producer for Walter Cronkite in Washington, D.C. Crystal and Chancellor, both with solid news backgrounds, came to New York from NBC's Chicago station, WMAQ, which since the early days of radio has been consistently innovative. These executives are backed by writers and reporters with worldwide experience, contributing to a professional approach to every story and the professional atmosphere of each telecast. Continuity is an important factor in broadcasting. In the news team's collective memory is an awareness of what happened yesterday, last week, and years ago. Each day begins where the previous one paused.

At 7:30 each morning, a number of story lists are prepared. The Shelf List shows perhaps several dozen short features on hand that can be aired at almost any time because they do not relate to specific news events. The subjects of the features are listed along with their precise running times in minutes: Supertankers (2:41), Siberian Pollution (3:02), Tennis (4:15), Hang Gliding (5:09). Another list shows the status of film and videotape news items that have been assigned in the United States and abroad and are expected to be available for this particular evening's news. Some are already in and comments indicate their

Because news events generally involve specific areas, and technical atlas-type maps would not provide good visual material for television, the graphics department prepares its own maps to highlight the exact locations of events (above). The newsfilm department contains its own complete lab for processing both color and black-and-white film, as well as for editing film (left).

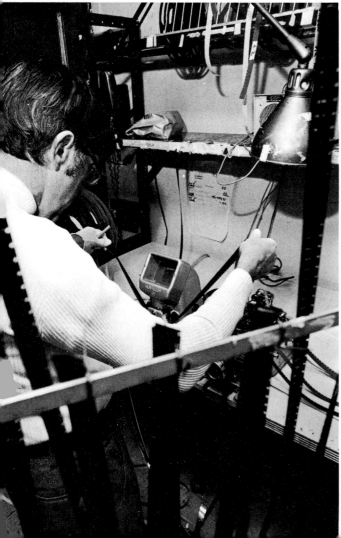

*Anchorman John Chancellor's day is longer than the time
he is on air. It begins in the morning and runs all
day, during which time he checks other media for news
and writes and edits much of his presentation. Only when
that is done can he calmly present the* Nightly News.

status: "needs script" or "trying despite bad film," "finishing this A.M.," or "trying for 1:15." Some may have been edited in the field or flown in as a reel of film or videotape, in which case the length of the reel is indicated in feet. The status is noted, for example: "1,200' (cut by *Today*)." In this case, film of a news story had been edited out of 1,200 feet of film and was probably used on *Today*. The *Nightly News* group would decide whether to reedit it or update it for the evening broadcast. Yet other stories are on their way to NBC and are noted with expected availability.

The longest early morning list concerns stories in the works in all eight NBC bureaus as well as in Europe and the Far East. The list, about fifty items long, is broken down by bureau, story, and reporter. As on the other lists, the status of every story is specified: "in house," or "due 10:15 processed," "assigned," "continues filming," perhaps "VTR [for videotape recording] due from Burbank," "editing and avail. London," "filming in London today, unknown if available for satellite," "aimed for satellite from Vienna." Added to this will be updating on developments that have occurred since the previous evening, or during this same morning in the distant time zones of Europe or the Middle East. (10:00 A.M. New York time is 3:00–5:00 P.M. in Europe, depending on the location; in the Far East it is tomorrow.)

After spending an hour or more assessing the status of the news, the news group assembles in Crystal's office about 11:45 for a conference call with NBC's domestic news bureaus, located in the five stations NBC owns (New York, Washington, D.C., Cleveland, Chicago, and Burbank), and in the cities of Atlanta, Houston, Miami, and again New York, which has another unit known as the Northeast Bureau. Each bureau reports its situation over the phone to Crystal; a small loudspeaker enables everyone to listen to the conversations. Then, with Crystal acting as moderator, the group develops a preliminary rundown of the news items that are most likely to be aired that particular evening. What follows is a description of how the news came together on one particular day, but it is typical of the process on any average day.

The *Nightly News* is broken down into five segments, usually with commercial breaks between each. There must be a balance between domestic and foreign news, live remotes alternating with other segments John Chancellor will do on camera, and perhaps a short feature. Some stories are ongoing, so the evening telecast will carry the latest developments with only a very brief introduction. Other stories are new; there may be a discussion as to what background is required to orient the viewer. The group watches a number of edited items on a monitor in Crystal's office, while a regular NBC daytime game show appears on a second monitor with the sound turned off.

Crystal asks that someone get London to telecopy the script to New York for a particular story that has been edited. From the script, it will be easy to tell what the item will look like without resorting to the costly process of relaying the audiovisual via satellite. That can be done quickly, later in the day, if it is decided the story will be used. Meantime, other items are coming in over the monitor and are subject to discussion and evaluation by the group.

The news group breaks for lunch by one o'clock. Elsewhere in the building, other activities are in progress relating to the *Nightly News*. The Newsfilm Department, which contains its own complete lab for processing both color and black-and-white film, receives a steady flow of film from around the world. Some of it is edited, some not; some has been processed, some not. All day long, different items are being cut and the voice narrative attached. Periodically, members of the news staff come to view completed stories and to check the progress of others in editing. When it is decided that a particular feature will go on the air that evening in a specific time slot, it is set up on a film projector that will direct the image into an electronic tube that automatically converts an optical picture into impulses that can be telecast. The projector has a code number and is wired into the control console in Studio 3-K. When the technical director of the *Nightly News* pushes its button, film will roll. A timing device is built into the circuit so that the projector comes on a few seconds in advance to get up to proper speed. Otherwise, the viewer would be greeted with the leader to the film (with optical markings . . . 6, 5, 4, 3, 2, 1, start) before the story itself came on the screen. Paralleling the film input is a steady flow of videotape items, which are similarly prepared and set up with cues so the director can roll them at a specific time.

At about 3:00 P.M., a second conference gets under-way in Les Crystal's office to review the rundown of the *Nightly News* items, segment by segment. Because the pattern of the developing news shifts throughout the day, contenders for air time that seemed strong in the morning may no longer have the same sense of urgency. Edited items have been exactly timed for length and are arranged within each segment both for continuing interest and time fit, along with specified times (twenty seconds, twenty-five seconds) for John Chancellor's introductions to live segments, and longer intervals (forty-five seconds, one minute) for those he will do on camera against an appropriate background. At the same time, graphics are identified. Two things are mentioned in this connection: the little viz and the big viz. Viz is short for "vizmo," a rear-projection technique. When Chancellor is presenting the news, there are three cameras on him. Viewed through one camera, he is seen head on. From another camera angle, the big viz appears behind him and to the right. In the view through the third camera, a console appears to the left with the small viz screen set in it, looking much like a small TV screen.

The conference breaks as the writers select items they feel especially comfortable with. "I'll take items three and eleven," says Chancellor. "I'll take nine and fourteen," says Millstein. Four news writers divide the remaining stories. Les Crystal moves out of his office and takes a seat where he can watch the monitors across the room, while at the same time scanning a series of last-minute teletypes handed to him. Chancellor, Millstein, and the writers are at their desks typing. At around five o'clock, a monitor shows several stories being relayed via satellite from London. At 5:30 David Brinkley's *Journal* comes in from Washington. Crystal and Fouhy are reading copy as it comes across their desks from the writers.

And the clock is ticking. The countdown is on for a broadcast less than an hour away. Instead of coming together and winding down now, however, there is every appearance that the *Nightly News* is coming apart; one grows increasingly conscious of the clock, and ultimately its big sweep second hand as well.

The key people at the small cluster of desks, including Chancellor a few feet to one side, are now asking questions of each other, or sometimes making remarks to no one in particular.

Crystal: "We actually have another spot where we left something out. How unusual!" He picks up a telephone. "Get me London, 743-8000, extension 4020, International Control Room. I want to speak to Irv Margolies, urgent. Hello, Irv? We've got lots of confusion here. What else have you fed [via satellite]? You fed the F-104? [Glancing at monitor while still skimming teletypes and scripts]. Here comes the Shah now. [The monitor shows Iran's chief of state arriving at a London airport.] Are we recording [this relay]? We're recording. Was the demonstration from Rome fed? I saw people marching in the streets [still skimming copy.]" His London conversation continues.

Several young women are typing cue sheets for the *Nightly News* rundown. These list each news item in order within the segments, give the precise length of each in minutes and seconds, locate the commercial breaks, how long they are and for what product, and list a continuing time log down the left-hand margin, beginning with 6:30:00 and ending with 6:58:15.

5:50

Crystal: Who's writing into Simpson [an introduction]?
Chancellor: I am.
Crystal: Who's writing into Pettit?
Chancellor: Gil is.
Crystal (glancing at monitor): Now the Rome demonstration is coming in. That was Rome that just came in, right?
Fouhy: Right.
Chancellor: Anybody got a Roosevelt Island script? Thanks.
Crystal (watching monitor again): What the hell's this?
Fouhy: That's Beirut.
Crystal: Do I have a Rowan script? Do we have a John Hart script?
Voice: Yes, we do.
Crystal: When am I going to get spot sheets on that damn voice-over? What about Simpson? What about Rowan? [A secretary tells him to pick up a telephone.] Yes? If you can do it, fine. If you can't, let us know. We're a minute forty seconds on Hart; ten seconds over on Pettit. Figure Pettit for a minute fifty?
Chancellor: Are we in trouble on time?
Crystal (watching the monitor again): Here comes the Harris stuff from Burbank now. That looks good.
Chancellor (to the group and looking up from a teletype): You want Mrs. Ford's poll figures? She's miles ahead of her husband, miles ahead.
Crystal: Let's drop Perez and put in defense on the big viz.
Voice: We dropped the big viz. How about a little viz?
Crystal: That's good enough. [Calls out to an assistant] I need you, Sandy. [To Fouhy, about a piece of copy] You are thirty seconds heavy, Ed.
Fouhy: Still thirty, eh?
Crystal: What's that tease going to show us?

6:15

John Chancellor has gotten up from his typewriter and is standing a few feet from Crystal's desk. He leans forward, puts his hands on the edge of the desk, and does a few standing push-ups. Then he heads for his office and on to the studio.

6:20

Voice: That's all from Los Angeles at this time.

Crystal: How much are we over?
Voice: Thirty.
Crystal: How did that happen?
Secretary: Les, you want to pick up Washington?
Fouhy: Hart is one minute fifty seconds. London holds together fine. Got a time for us on Pettit?

6:25

Despite the apparent confusion, the *Nightly News* is ready to go on the air. These people are all professionals. Moreover, they know one another extremely well. On any given afternoon, each also knows exactly what the others are doing, for what they are putting together is a single entity: the *Nightly News.* Although the show may consist of several dozen news items, it is a microcosm of what is going on in the nation and throughout the world. This huddle of people sits in the center of a global spiderweb with innumerable filaments carrying messages and vibrations. To manage the mass of information, they must work collectively, talking together and passing copy back and forth throughout the day. In this way the team becomes a collective perception of the news.

Electronic journalism is complex. There is a multitude of details that must be set precisely: which viz shows what and when, which remote comes in at what spot, what film or videotape item is cued where (and is it ready?). Since the show is telecast live, there is no time to correct mistakes. The group cross-checks itself, and, in this sense, what each person is doing is everyone else's business. The product is a cohesive evening outlook on a vast and complicated world.

By 6:26 the news is effectively buttoned up. Though it will be seen live in most of the Eastern United States shortly, it is also taped. WNBC-TV in New York and several other stations run the *Nightly News* at 7:00 P.M. It is also transmitted to the West for later use because of the time difference. If, in the next three hours, there is a major news development, Burbank can open up the taped show and add items as required. Crystal, Millstein, and Fouhy leave the newsroom and take the elevator down to Studio 3-K. The professionals, the news group and the technical people who support it, have done their work. Everything is cued into the studio control room. There the director and his associates have at their fingertips a highly sophisticated electronic console that governs the entire telecast. Alertness and technical expertise can correct and even anticipate a mistake. A newscaster can be instructed to ad-lib or slow down, a commercial message can be reslotted to a different spot, even the order of the show's elements can be changed if there is a malfunction in a film or tape feed.

The big second hand sweeps toward 6:30. The director jabs a finger, the opening titles appear, followed by John Chancellor. He looks up pleasantly at the camera and says, in his relaxed but upbeat voice: "Good evening."

MTP, as it's known within NBC, is the oldest of all network television programs. Over the years, it has proved to be broadcasting's most authoritative and influential public affairs presentation. Millions of Americans hear it on Sunday afternoons on about four hundred stations of the NBC television and radio networks and in twenty-nine countries abroad via the American Forces Radio and Television Service. Many governmental officials and opinion molders watch the program, including, according to a recent survey, nine out of ten Congressmen.

The format is simple. A moderator and four top journalists question their Sunday guest in an unrehearsed news conference. Guests are leading figures currently in the news: heads of state, government officials, diplomatic and military officers, business and labor leaders, scientists, educators, champions of causes such as civil rights, the environment, or women's lib. Because the questioning is both timely and topical, the show frequently generates Monday morning's news headlines.

Meet the Press was inaugurated in 1945 as a radio promotion for *American Mercury* magazine. It was the creation of the magazine's publisher and editor, Lawrence E. Spivak. Two years later, when it moved to NBC television, Spivak continued his role as producer and moderator of the show. "The show's early prominence," according to *Time* magazine, "came from Spivak's uncanny knack for snaring newsmakers while they were hot, and from the tough questions he threw at them once they were on the air." The AFL-CIO chieftain George Meany, veteran debater, once growled, "A half hour on that show can age you ten years." Another observer of the MTP grillings commented: "Politicians consider the program to be the most formidable of all the news programs, and they confess to me they do more homework for it than for any other on television."

After nearly thirty years as chief interrogator, Lawrence Spivak retired. But *Meet the Press* continues and maintains his unswerving dedication to ferreting out facts.

Around three o'clock on the bitter cold morning of January 14, 1952, NBC Producer Mort Werner left his New York apartment to look for a cab. On the street, with his hat pulled down and collar turned up, he aroused the suspicions of a police officer. "What are you doing here?"

"I work for NBC. We're doing a new television show starting at seven this morning."

Prior to that time, network programming had usually begun at the more leisurely hour of noon. The officer's response was understandable: "Television at seven o'clock in the morning? You must be out of your mind!"

The producer's destination was the now-defunct RCA Exhibition Hall in New York City, located on the south side of Forty-ninth Street opposite the towering RCA Building and just a few steps from Rockefeller Plaza with its ice-skating rink. The hall had huge floor-to-ceiling glass windows on the street and passersby could see everything inside. Prior to January 14, it had featured an exhibition of the latest RCA television equipment and other RCA communications devices. Television was still in its infancy, and the general public was just becoming acquainted with the new medium. Visitors to New York City formed a continuous parade through the hall, which featured among other things a slightly elevated platform on which one or several people could stand in front of a television camera. They could see themselves on a nearby monitor. People on the street could do the same, watching several monitors close to the big windows. For the debut of the *Today* show, all that changed. The hall was converted to a large studio with futuristic world hemispheres linked together with a mind-boggling maze of electronic wiring, including a series of large clock faces arranged at intervals to show time zones.

Putting on a two-hour early morning television show

Meet the Press *during the 50s:*
In 1950 the panel included
Messrs. Riesel, Brooks, McNeil,
and Davis—the guest with
Mr. Spivak is James Roosevelt;
in 1954 the show questioned
a young Massachusetts senator.

was not only a novelty; it was also a gamble for the network. Dave Garroway was selected to be the first host of *Today.* Garroway was a well-known pioneer, coming from what is now referred to nostalgically as the Chicago School of TV. The Chicago School of TV had certain definable characteristics, according to a long-time student of the subject, Professor Joel Sternberg, of the University of Illinois. It was experimental, visual, intimate, and usually live, so that one never knew in advance quite what to expect on the air. A group of people created theatrical marvels on minuscule budgets. The approach was quite different from that being taken at the television centers on the East and West coasts, which generally attempted to convert their own local artistic environments into some form suitable for TV. Writing in *Theater Arts,* in 1951, Arch Oboler, producer and writer of the old radio mystery show *Lights Out,* commented: "While Hollywood rushes to film, and New York frantically tries to force the theater through the cathode tube, Chicago alone has recognized a new art form in the television medium." This recognition was a spill-over from the earlier Chicago radio school where, as Oboler noted, "Chicago radio discovered that the listener was as close to the performer as the microphone was to the performer." Thus performers could literally whisper into the listener's ear, producing an intimacy that, with appropriate sound effects, was the key to the chilling success of *Lights Out, Inner Sanctum,* and other mystery and adventure serials. The Chicago School of Television also encouraged performers to treat their audiences as if they were only a few feet distant.

The three most memorable shows from the Chicago School were *Studs' Place; Kukla, Fran and Ollie;* and *Garroway at Large.* Both *Studs' Place* and *Garroway at Large* were the creations of a former advertising copywriter named Charlie Andrews. There were no scripts in either show, just subject-matter outlines of a page or two. Kukla and Ollie were puppets, controlled by Burr Tillstrom, and Fran was Fran Allison, who stood on the stage and spoke to the two puppets. *Kukla, Fran and Ollie* was also done impromptu.

Garroway at Large originated from NBC's small studio in Chicago's Merchandise Mart and featured vocalists, an orchestra, and guests. Dave Garroway roamed the studio, leading the audience from one situation or set to another. During his wanderings, Garroway would occasionally give brief discourses on zany subjects, such as the ruby-polishing industry in Siam or the construction of eleven-foot poles for touching people you wouldn't touch with ten-foot poles. Sometimes stagehands added or removed scenery behind people who were performing. White Sox slugger of the day, Eddie Robinson, struck out at screwballs that came whistling across the stage in a corkscrew pattern several feet in diameter. Sometimes the cameras wandered around the stage, looking at each other. Garroway, aside from being a natural and ingenious host and interviewer, was a showman (his production crew included two magicians). He had a closing line for each program that began: "This program came to you from Chicago, where—." At that point he might add, "even pigs can whistle." On one occasion, the tag was "where people can trust each other." Then Garroway turned around to reveal a dagger embedded in his back.

The novelty and intimacy couldn't save the Chicago School. Advertising agencies were now paying television's biggest bills, and most agencies were headquartered in New York or Los Angeles. As *Time* magazine observed in the fall of 1951, "with large sums at stake, they prefer to have their programs produced and staged close at hand where they can keep a firm finger in the pie." In consequence, Dave Garroway was himself soon at large.

Then he and Charlie Andrews were called to New York to discuss the *Today* show.

When *Today* first went on the air, some reviewers thought it wasn't much of anything. Commented one, ". . . an incredible two-hour comedy of errors, perpetrated as a 'new kind of television.'" Another wrote acidly that *Today* was "something without which TV can do very nicely."

One reason the show was a shambles was its technical complexity. In many ways, it was patterned on the *Garroway at Large* show, with the host wandering into and out of one or another interview, news break, or entertainment scene. These segments had to be set up in advance and cued on the air with precise timing. Often, a segment would be remote (such as a political interview from Washington, D.C.), presenting new difficulties. *Today* was a directorial and electronic nightmare.

Gradually the show shook down and woke up. When *Today* first went on the air in 1952, it was seen in twenty-six cities in nineteen states and the District of Columbia. At present, it can be seen in nearly every TV home in the continental United States and wakes up more than 6.5 million daily viewers. It has become television's longest-running weekday program.

In addition to entertainment, *Today* presents the news and weather each half hour, is on top of fast-breaking stories during the morning hours, and adds features on contemporary issues.

Because of both its time slot and its timeliness, *Today* numbers many members of Congress and government officials among its viewers. Lyndon Johnson, when he was president, was a faithful viewer. He was interested both in how his administration was covered and in what influenced people. From time to time, he would call to speak with someone who had just been interviewed, on one occasion inviting Jack Dempsey to visit him at the White House. From a shaky start, *Today* has become an American institution, one that has changed the viewing habits of many people. Commented Jack Gould in *The New York Times,* "The gymnastic secret that apparently makes *Today* an institution is to keep one foot in Pennsylvania Avenue and the other in Shubert Alley."

One of the ingredients that helped get the show off the ground in the early years was the acquisition by Garroway of a side man, a second banana to the top banana in the form of a naturally banana-loving young chimp with the name of J. Fred Muggs. Aside from getting into things, messing up scripts, spilling stuff, and occasionally escaping, J. Fred could be counted on to mug it up magnificently on camera, suggesting that the intent behind the name was: J. Fred mugs. Crowds of people on the way to work would gather to watch the show through the big glass windows, and the street outside gradually became an extension of the studio within. The cameras were sometimes turned on the curbside audience to catch people displaying signs with messages for the folks at home or greetings to members of the show's cast. For many weeks, a city baker had his truck drive round and round the block in hopes that his sign would get on TV. Occasionally, Garroway conducted man-on-the-street interviews. Bob and Ray came on the show and did a fake sidewalk interview. One celebrated interviewee on several occasions was President Harry S. Tru-

*In the Miami Beach Convention Hall, NBC housed
radio studios, a complete TV transmitting
station, newsrooms, three mobile units connected
to cameras within the hall, videotape
facilities, and a master TV control system.*

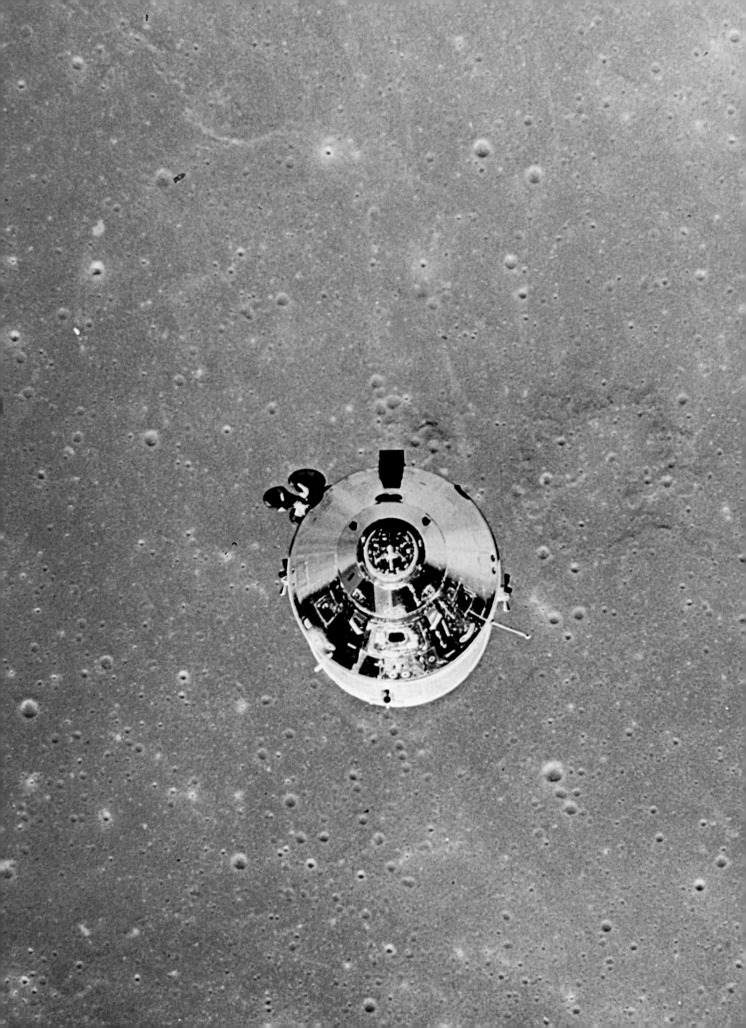

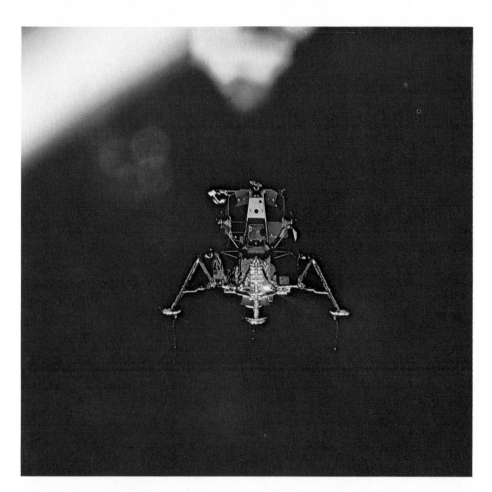

Opposite: View of Apollo Command
Module as seen from Lunar
Module. Armstrong and Aldrin in
the LEM have separated and
are preparing to go to the moon's
surface. *Left:* The Lunar
Module after separation and
before touchdown. *Below:*
Finally, splashdown and recovery.

Clockwise from left: Co-hosts until the summer of 1976 of the Today *show, Barbara Walters and Jim Hartz;* NBC White Paper: Migrant, *a documentary with Chet Huntley that focused on migrant labor in Florida; NBC documentary* An Island Called Ellis; *NBC newsman and commentator Edwin Newman;* Nightly News *anchorman John Chancellor.*

man. Truman was well known for his brisk, early morning constitutionals. When in New York, he customarily stayed at the Waldorf Astoria, a few blocks across town from Radio City. His morning tours sometimes brought him along Forty-ninth Street, accompanied by an entourage of panting reporters and Secret Servicemen.

When dignitaries and heads of state appeared on *Today,* a red carpet was rolled out to the street, and Garroway ceremoniously escorted the guest inside. On one occasion, an incredible contraption called the Green Monster appeared at curbside. It was a jet-propelled car, and its pilot, Art Arfons, was on hand to explain how he had set a world land-speed record in 1965. And at the height of "Muggs mania" in the mid fifties, a man turned up on the street wearing a gorilla outfit and carrying a sign that said "I'm J. Fred Muggs' long lost brother." The temptation proved irresistible to the cameras, which focused in for a close-up of the sign. Whereupon the gorilla promptly flipped it. Viewers of *Today* saw a new legend: "Tonight watch King Kong on Channel 9."

One early mainstay of *Today,* which has been carried over in the two-hour Bicentennial visits every Friday to one of the American states, was the idea of taking the audience to different places. The show's first trip abroad, in 1957, took viewers to Canada. In 1959, a week-long visit to Paris was a rare treat. American audiences enjoyed Brigitte Bardot, the Arc de Triomphe, sidewalk cafés, and the world-famous Parisian restaurant, *La Tour d'Argent,* where the head chef gave a meticulous demonstration of how a renowned *spécialité de la maison,* pressed duck, was prepared. As the chef described the process with typical Gallic verve, his comments were immediately translated into English. Mobile video equipment and transatlantic jet service (inaugurated by BOAC in 1957) made it possible for Americans to view the taped features only a day later.

Unfortunately, around the same time as the visit to France, the *Today* show had introduced what was to become a regular feature of the program: the live commercial. Immediately following the segment with the chef, Garroway was handed a pot of boiling water and a swatch of carpet made from a new synthetic fiber. He dunked the swatch dramatically into the pot to demonstrate the carpet material's durability. Mistaking this for some typically mindless American parody of his work, the Paris chef stalked off in a rage, muttering about the desecraters of his art and his restaurant.

Today had other run-ins with the French. In 1965, it became the first regularly scheduled show to be relayed entirely by satellite, in this case the newly launched *Early Bird.* The program featured segments from England, France, Holland, and Italy, all coordinated from a control room in Brussels, Belgium. At one point, the American coordinating director in Brussels asked that the French director assigned to the Paris mobile unit take some time and rehearse his segment before it went on the air. Snapped the Frenchman haughtily, "Rehearse some other country; the French do not need rehearsal!"

Following the success of the first Paris visit, *Today's* crew took its viewers to Rome, England, the Netherlands, Puerto Rico, New Orleans for Mardi Gras week, New York for the World's Fair of 1964, the Virgin Islands, and numerous other vacation spots. The show also interviewed people at home: Princess Grace of Monaco and Dwight and Mamie Eisenhower on their fiftieth wedding anniversary, on the Gettysburg farm. They also covered Jacqueline Kennedy's 1962 goodwill tour of India. This last was the first major on-air assignment for a promising reporter, Barbara Walters.

At its inception, *Today* was considered to be entertainment and was produced within the NBC Program Department, even though it featured news and weather in its regular format. Consequently, the hosts and other regulars on the show found nothing improper in personally doing or introducing live commercials. A great many sponsors and ad agencies came to feel that their products got an extra sales boost by being pitched live by the show's personalities. This practice became institutionalized, sponsors expected it, and it was a key element in the commercial appeal and hence the success of the show. Later on, *Today* was brought under the aegis of NBC News and John Chancellor was nominated to host it. Chancellor, professional journalist to the core, followed the credo that doing commercials represented a conflict of interest that might undermine his reputation for objectivity, and he did not do the commercials. When Chancellor left the show, NBC News relented in this instance, and *Today* went back to its traditional live pitches, with Hugh Downs as host.

One of the reasons for *Today's* continuing dominance of the early morning hours is the fact that the show is very much a "now" show. And one of the reasons for that has been Stuart Schulberg, who became the show's producer in 1968 and was named executive producer in 1971. Now a producer of NBC news specials, Schulberg started as a newspaper reporter and writer, then turned to producing television documentaries and feature films. Under Schulberg, getting *Today* together became a bit like "trying to stuff a hurricane into a paper bag every morning," as he was fond of putting it.

Before Schulberg took over as *Today's* producer, relative calm was the order of the day. Interviews, features, and special events were scheduled as long as a month in advance. Changes were made only when extraordinary news events occurred. Otherwise, goings-on in the nation and around the world were mainly covered in the four segments of news and weather the show carries each half hour. Schulberg changed all that, to the point where the show could, as he put it, "turn on a dime". He, his second in command—producer Douglas Sinsel—and Gene Farinet, the news producer, would sometimes confer by phone as late as midnight, if something very significant were breaking in the news. Often they made changes in the show overnight, so that when 7:00 A.M. came, *Today* was there with the very latest on what was happening. The show continues to retain this last-minute flexibility. Often key people return to headquarters during the evening, or over a weekend, to assemble an hour special for the next morning—or a whole new show for that matter. Moreover, the new show, or segment of it, does not have to come from New York. It can originate from anywhere the network can put together an electronic tie-in. With satellite relays now a standard part of *Today's* operations, this means practically anywhere in the world.

Artists, writers, entertainers, and especially government officials, diplomats, politicians, and even presidents, are all eager to appear on the program. It can do a lot to promote a book or enhance a performer's image and familiarity in the public eye. People in and around government vie with one another to appear in connection with a timely issue or a favorite cause. One reason for this eagerness is that they know others of their kind watch the show, and will

President Lyndon Johnson showed viewers around his corner of Texas in The Hill Country: Lyndon Johnson's Texas. *Filming of the show provided a host of inside stories for years afterward.*

121

be listening to their point of view. More importantly, perhaps, is the fact that they understand the main audience the show attracts. That audience is not found principally in our major urban centers, where big metropolitan daily newspapers can be counted on to cover the political and cultural scene extensively. Rather, it lies in the smaller cities—those with populations of under half a million people—and in the even smaller towns, where newspaper coverage tends to be weak.

Stuart Schulberg and his associates are well aware of how influential their show is. And they make every effort to air as varied a cornucopia of views and news and entertainment as they can assemble. Technology, of course, helps. But it is the staff that makes the show what it is. That includes the quartet that goes on camera with it, the "talent" as they are called, as well as some seventy other people. Half a dozen writers produce material for the program's hosts. Today also has two directors, three unit managers to handle budgets and logistics, several film editors, and a copy editor. There are a number of production assistants,

researchers, and coordinators, too. The Washington unit has its own producer, writer, and correspondent. There was a separate Bicentennial unit, complete with producer, associate producer, production assistant, unit manager, writer, and researcher. And there are a producer and assistant just for the commercials. Getting the news together involves still another subdivision within the show, a night news editor, and four staff writers.

The heart of this function is the network news center, a huge, loftlike room with banks of teletype machines, rows of TV monitors, and other electric and electronic input-output devices. The center is manned by several dozen people who sort out the input—printed matter, videotapes, satellite relays—and earmark it for the news group that requires it: the Nightly News, NBC Radio, NBC-owned stations and affiliates, and the Today show. There is constant communication among the various groups within NBC concerned with presenting the news, so that each knows what the other is doing. Thus, a late-breaking item that John Chancellor covered on the Nightly News with many details still missing at air time, might appear in more complete form as the first news feature on the Today show.

Whatever the next morning brings, still more people will be involved. For the staff also includes a set designer, graphic artists (on duty both day and night), a talent coordi-

nator, a property manager (for props), a book coordinator, who reviews all current writers' production, a stage manager, and a scenic designer. The habitat of these individuals is an L-shaped cluster of several dozen small, cluttered offices, cubicles, and work areas. It looks very much like a news operation, and like the Nightly News area, it belies the national reach that resides there.

This continual and complex interplay of people produces a remarkably varied show, a "movable feast" that moves all around the country and all over the world to deliver at air time. In a single year, 1975, Today interviewed 800 people, including 65 Senators, 50 Congressmen, 20 Cabinet members, 20 governors, and 200 authors. It also telecast 100 satellite feeds, 75 from Europe and 25 from Asia. The transportation for its various staffers roaming the world included orders for: hydrofoil, horses, mule, kayak, jeep, hay-cutter, farm tractor, motorcycle, helicopter, as well as more conventional rental vehicles. The Bicentennial unit traveled 130,000 miles to cover twenty-six states. Jim Hartz took 130 air flights to join the unit in most of these

states. Reporter Barbara Walters went to China and Cuba.

The Today show has, for nearly a quarter century, presented a veritable cavalcade of events both in America and abroad, holding up a mirror to a world that seems to spin just a little faster each year. The program has proved to be the most durable daily show on the air. When one looks at Today, one must conclude that the seemingly grandiose idea was not far off after all. The show is nearly everything to everyone. If the technical complications seemed insurmountable in January, 1952, in retrospect they are what Jackie Gleason humorously refers to as "a mere bag of shells" by today's Today standards.

Compared to the modern version of Today, *the early show was something of a shambles. Host Dave Garroway wandered into and out of one or another interview, news break, or entertainment scene. Passersby could stop and stare in at the show. These pictures are from the first telecast.*

Ten-Ton Pencils
Documentaries

When television was introduced, it seemed logical that documentaries would prove an admirable subject for the new visual medium. Documentary motion pictures had already demonstrated widespread appeal, notably in such classics as Robert Flaherty's Eskimo feature *Nanook of the North* and Pare Lorentz's *The Plow That Broke the Plains*, which traced the source of the great dust bowls of the thirties. Hollywood had also struck gold with *The Grapes of Wrath* (from John Steinbeck's novel about uprooted Okies). Europeans had scored with such "neorealist" films as *Open City* and *The Bicycle Thief*. Nevertheless, there were doubts about the relative worth of producing serious documentary films for the television audience.

"Cumbersome and expensive," grumbled NBC's Fred Freed, who would later raise the documentary to the level of an art. Two CBS partners, who had teamed up in 1946 to produce the memorable radio programs *Hear It Now*, and would go on to add sight to sound in their celebrated *See It*

Now television series, were equally dubious.

"A ten-ton pencil," said Fred Friendly.

"I wish we could disinvent it," commented Edward R. Murrow.

"Just to do a documentary in those days was something," recalls Reuven Frank, the dean of NBC documentarians, currently the producer of *Weekend*. "Even an interview was an achievement, because it took a half ton of equipment to record it."

The problem was the unwieldy 35-mm black-and-white movie camera in use at the time. Early television cameras were cumbersome too, of course, but they were usually confined to studios, where they could be manipulated with rea-

East Berlin West Berlin

Opposite far left: One of the first documentaries being made, the comprehensive study of the mammoth St. Lawrence project. Opposite right, left, and below: In 1962 NBC released The Tunnel, an actual filming of the digging of, and use for escape of, a tunnel that went from West Berlin to East Berlin.

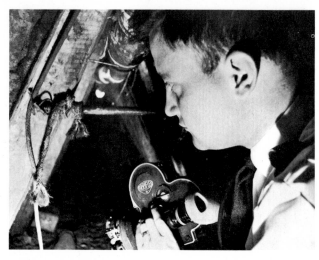

Top and above: The film of tunnel-digging and escape was authentic because most of the documentary was shot in damp, cramped conditions, with a few light bulbs for illumination. Opposite: The Battle of Newburgh was a probe of welfare problems and corruption in upstate Newburgh, New York.

sonable ease. Producing a documentary required lugging all that 35-mm equipment, including heavy electrical cable and conspicuous microphones, from one location to another. Once on the scene, it took some time to set up. Whatever spontaneity those being interviewed might have had would have evaporated by the time the crew was ready to shoot.

Nevertheless, many newsreel crews became first-rate documentary teams. In those days, documentary producers enjoyed an autonomy unique in network news. Each one became, in effect, a pioneer who followed his own bent.

A technological breakthrough made the production of documentaries more feasible. Sixteen-millimeter cameras and film were perfected to the point where they could almost match the 35-mm quality. The lighter, smaller film and equipment brought a real revolution in flexibility, mobility, and ease of operation to TV journalism.

Reuven Frank believes that "the best documentaries are accidents." One interesting accident happened in Germany. An NBC News cameraman, Gary Stindt, found a 350-mm telephoto lens in a pawnshop. During 1952 and 1953 he spent many hours atop a bakery, where he could look down on the grounds of Spandau prison, which housed several former Nazis sentenced after the Nuremberg war criminals trials. Stindt's attention was drawn to one inmate strolling in a garden. He began to film the man, who turned out to be the notorious Rudolf Hess. Hess had been a high Nazi official. During the war, he escaped in an airplane and parachuted into Scotland to present a wild scheme for making peace with the Allies. Reuven Frank later wove Stindt's footage with other material into an award-winning exploration of Nazism called *The Road to Spandau*.

Another dramatic event occurred in Berlin during 1961 and 1962. A small group of West German students, determined to liberate friends from East Germany, surreptitiously approached NBC's Berlin staff. They needed funds for various kinds of equipment. Two young German photographers who were working for NBC, Klaus and Peter Dehmel, were determined to film the whole operation. The project was ambitious, to say the least: digging a tunnel from an unused basement in a West German building near the Berlin Wall all the way under the wall and across to another cellar in East Berlin. The operation took months, came close to disaster on a number of occasions, and near detection by the East German police, who reputedly shot escapees first and asked questions later. Incredibly, fifty-nine men, women, and children were rescued before a broken water main flooded the tunnel. The brothers had the epic on film, every foot of it wet, dirty, and hair-raising. The quality was terrible. The film had been shot in damp, cramped conditions, with a few light bulbs for illumination. Its authenticity was, in fact, one of its strengths. Reuven Frank held a special screening of *The Tunnel* for the NBC management. They agreed to air it, even though the State Department had objected, suggesting that it might damage East-West relations and jeopardize the lives of those who had escaped. NBC held a special screening in Berlin for the escapees and blacked out the faces of those who requested it. Then, late in 1962, NBC released *The Tunnel*. Because it had become a global news event, it captured a huge audience.

Among NBC documentarians, Fred Freed, a former radio journalist, had a special talent for interviewing people. He also had a strong suit in compiling solid data on important issues. In *The Decision to Drop the Bomb* (1965), he

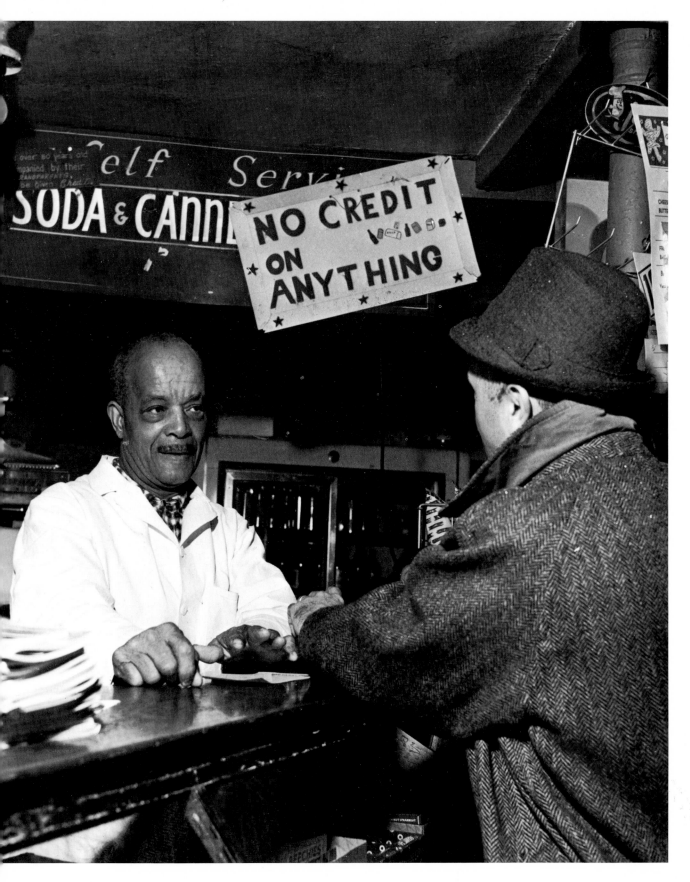

Preceding pages: In 1962 NBC received permission
to bring cameras into the USSR. The result was The Kremlin,
which included views of, among other things, the
Kremlin and St. Basil's Cathedral. A year later producer
Lucy Jarvis filmed The Louvre, hosted by Charles Boyer.
Viewers were taken through the great art museum—the
preparations were painstaking, expensive, and exacting.

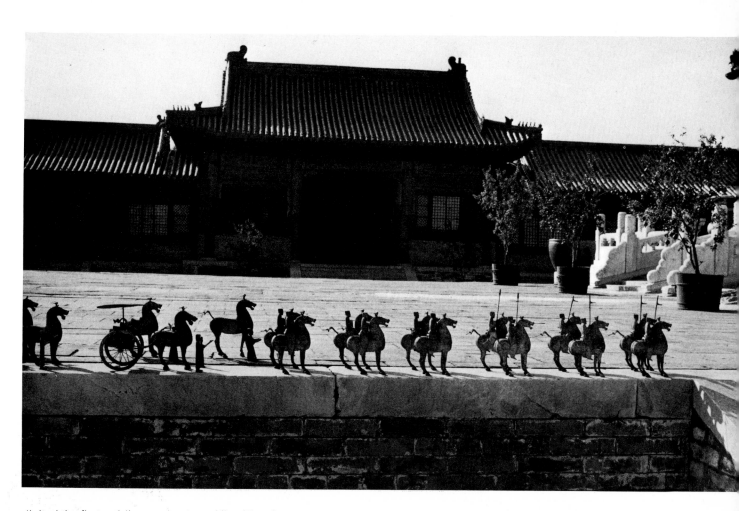

elicited the first public comments on Hiroshima from members of the wartime Japanese government. Getting officials to talk freely for any documentary is not easy. Freed once noted that "the principals in world events often won't talk, or will give the official version, or are saving stuff for their memoirs."

Another young documentarian, Al Wasserman, filmed the first NBC investigative documentary, a probe of welfare problems and official corruption in Newburgh, New York. It was titled *The Battle of Newburgh* and led to a wide public outcry against such abuses.

Still another documentary pioneer, Lou Hazam, staked out the world of art and culture as his domain. Using a subjective camera approach, he did the life of Jesus in *The Way of the Cross*, Van Gogh in *Vincent Van Gogh: A Self-Portrait*, as well as other classical subjects. A particularly beautiful example of his work was *The River Nile* (1962), with James Mason as the narrator. Hazam took his viewers on a leisurely and colorful trip down that great and historic river, from its origins high in the legendary "Mountains of the Moon" (the Ruwenzori, on the border between Zaire and Uganda) north through the Sudan and Egypt, to its great delta on the Mediterranean. Along the way, viewers were treated to views of the fabulous flora and fauna of the river, many of its peoples (including the strikingly tall Watusi), and the basin's ancient historic sites, some of which were threatened by inundation when the Aswan Dam was built.

Over at CBS, documentaries were also achieving suc-

After a decade of negotiations, Jarvis managed to film yet another forbidden place, this time the Forbidden City in the People's Republic of China. Opposite: Jarvis (next to camera) and crew above a portrait of Chairman Mao on the Gate of Heavenly Peace at the main entrance to the Forbidden City in Peking. Above: Unearthed relics discovered in 1969—bronze horses from a general's tomb—posed before the Forbidden City.

Below: U.S.S. Shaw exploding at Pearl Harbor, a scene from Victory at Sea, a 26-week series, scored by Richard Rodgers, that depicted the United States Navy during World War II. Right: Joseph Valachi, being kept safe by incarceration, as he appeared in the American White Paper: Organized Crime in the U.S. Opposite: Moses with the tablets of the law, from the Rembrandt Staatliche Museum in Berlin, which was filmed for a Project 20 show, The Law and the Prophets.

cess, notably with the launching of Ed Murrow's *See It Now*. When Murrow confronted and exposed the sham of Senator Joseph McCarthy's anti-Communist witch-hunt, a milestone in investigative reporting was reached.

Throughout the 1950s documentaries were aired in what was then known as the "intellectual ghetto": Saturday and Sunday afternoons. Even then, they could be bumped by anything else that network executives considered more important.

Just before the Cuban missile crisis, NBC producer George Vicas went to Moscow to do *The Kremlin*. It was the first time that ancient seat of Russian authority was opened to a foreign news organization. Vicas produced an incredible portrait of Russia through the centuries with its czars and serfs, autocracy and communism. Court intrigues were covered as were the murderous life of Ivan the Terrible,

Napoleon's predations, and the great revolution that made the USSR what it is.

That NBC got into the Kremlin was due to the tenacity, guile, and persuasiveness of the associate producer, Lucy Jarvis. Unbeknownst to her and the rest of the crew, the Cuban missile crisis was occurring while *The Kremlin* was being filmed. As Lucy tells the story, President Kennedy, after the crisis had been resolved, joked that "Khrushchev promised to get his missiles out of Cuba, if I promised to get Lucy out of the Kremlin."

Two years later (1964) Lucy wangled her way into filming the Louvre, in Paris. Charles Boyer took NBC viewers through the greatest art museum in the world, delving into its past and the sources of its treasures. The climax of the show included a revelation of what happened when the Germans invaded Paris early in World War II.

When the enemy reached the famous museum, it was utterly empty of anything of value. The French had packed up all their art treasures and carted them away to the countryside. The contents of the Louvre were hidden in barns and cellars, by farmers, merchants, and chateau owners. The Nazis found much wine, but in the Louvre they found nothing. When the war was over, the art was returned, and not one piece was missing.

After a decade of patient negotiations, Lucy Jarvis was permitted to enter yet another forbidden place, this time *The Forbidden City* in the People's Republic of China. During the sixties, Ted Yates, a courageous journalist and producer, took great personal risks to document the struggles in the Congo, Vietnam, and Laos. He lost his life covering the outbreak of the Arab-Israeli war of 1967. Another NBC filmmaker, Martin Carr, revealed the plight of farm workers, in *Migrant* (1970), despite threats from growers and local officials. Eliot Frankel produced *Pensions: The Broken Promise* (1972), and NBC had to go to court to defend, successfully, the editorial judgments that the show reflected.

In 1965, before ecology became a household word, Gerald Green was exploring the wonders of the Grand Canyon and the Colorado River with famed naturalist Joseph Wood Krutch. Two years earlier, in *The Problem with Water . . . Is People,* Reuven Frank had studied the problems of diverting that celebrated river's waters for irrigation in the Southwest. Craig Fisher took a look at ecological questions in *The Everglades* and *The American Wilderness.* Another long-time NBC documentarian, Robert "Shad" Northshield, who earlier had examined problems of adoption in *The Chosen Child,* did a two-and-a-half hour survey of the sixties, called *From Here to the Seventies.* Among his other reports were *The Sins of the Fathers* (1973), about racially mixed orphans in Vietnam, which launched a storm of mail to the network, and, more recently, three Bicentennial specials narrated by David Brinkley: *Life, Liberty,* and *The Pursuit of Happiness.*

In 1963, NBC did something unique in documentary history. The network preempted three hours of prime time for a special on the civil rights struggle: *The American Revolution of '63.* With the single exception of an ABC special on Africa, only NBC has offered evening-long documentaries on this scale. The practice continues when a subject of sufficient importance and complexity warrants it.

Still other forms have been found for the documentary. In 1955, NBC produced a show anchored by Dave Garroway called *Wide Wide World.* It was designed to demonstrate just what television could do and featured remotes from many parts of the United States and the Caribbean. Some years later came the first of many NBC *White Papers,* examining subjects of specific and timely national interest. One of the most memorable of all NBC documentary achievements, and one of the earliest, was a series called *Project 20,* which began with a twenty-six-week series prelude, in the 1951-52 season. *Victory at Sea* depicted the triumphs of the United States Navy during World War II and featured a music score by Richard Rodgers. The subsequent

Project 20 shows were an hour long, and they received good sponsorship into the mid sixties.

What the *Project 20* (for twentieth century) unit would do was clearly stated at the outset by the producer, Henry Salamon: ". . . study the events, the mass movements, the wars, the life, the mores . . . and . . . place all this history in perspective, so that Twentieth Century man would have the opportunity to re-examine the road he has traveled and gauge where he is going." The development of the atomic bomb was explored in *Three, Two, One—Zero.* Other historical events covered included the rise of communism in the USSR and the rise and fall of Adolf Hitler (*The Twisted Cross*). Shows like *The Jazz Age* and *Life in the Thirties* (narrated by Fred Allen) covered life and mores. Programs like *Meet Mr. Lincoln, The Coming of Christ,* and *Mark Twain's America* recreated men and events.

Under the immediate direction of assistant producer Donald Hyatt—who later became their producer—*Project 20* shows were lovingly and artistically put together, winning many awards at film festivals both in the United States and abroad (Edinburgh and Venice, among others). Almost all the regular *Project 20* shows had original musical scores by Robert Russell Bennett, known elsewhere for his fine arrangements of musicals for Rodgers and Hammerstein, Cole Porter, Irving Berlin, and others. At the outset, Bennett took Richard Rodgers's thematic material for *Victory at Sea* and produced a soaring score from it.

Nearly all the *Project 20* scripts were written by Richard Hanser. Critics repeatedly remarked on their quality. They are now at the University of Wisconsin Center for Theater Research. The unit did four years of pictorial research for a single show, *End of the Trail,* about the destruction of the Plains Indians. Walter Brennan narrated it. For *The West of Charles Russell,* about America's greatest Western artist, the unit combed the country from Montana to Texas and located several thousand of his paintings, as well as numerous old photographs. To bring them to life *Project 20* introduced to TV a technique called still-pictures-in-motion, zooming in on details, panning, drawing back, and intercutting to give a sense of motion. This technique has been used to good advantage in many historical shows. Composer Bennett was so impressed by Charles Russell's art that he wrote:

Charles M. Russell, the cow-boy artist,
And what an artist he be;
If Picasso had had a lasso,
He might have painted as well as he.
That's how it seems to me.

That sort of affection was characteristic of the *Project 20* unit. The shows were *very* expensive to produce, and they were historically accurate. *The Real West,* for example, narrated by the late Gary Cooper, showed Americans what a scruffy, no-good lot of characters most of our Western heroes actually were. Prints of the shows are treasured today, and the National Archives has a complete collection.

"It's Howdy Doody Time"

Children's Shows

hildren are our most important national resource. Since the early days of radio, NBC has felt a serious obligation to produce programs that would interest, entertain, and inform young people. NBC became the first network to have a vice-president exclusively in charge of children's programming. Yet for all its concern and careful planning, the network has had to alter its programming focus more than once. Children's shows have become some of the most difficult to produce in terms of content, and, as might be expected, some of the most important shows are those produced for children.

In the early days of TV, putting on shows to entertain kids was a fairly simple matter—or so it seems in retrospect. The very first was *Howdy Doody*, which went on the air in 1947 and had an amazingly long run—until 1960. Howdy Doody was a puppet, the creation of a disc jockey from Buffalo, New York, named Bob Smith. Bob came to New York City and invented a new personality for himself, Buffalo Bob. Howdy the puppet was an all-American boy with a shock of red hair, freckles, a big grin, and eyes agog with wonder, a cut in intelligence above that rube dummy, Mortimer Snerd, which Edgar Bergen had created as a companion piece to his sharp, sassy Charlie McCarthy. Howdy's habitat was a small stage, which occasionally featured other puppets. Buffalo Bob presided in front of the stage, and in back or to the side of him was the peanut gallery, a

box that accommodated about thirty youngsters. The show opened with all the kids singing, enthusiastically, "It's Howdy Doody Time," a tune every moppet in America must have ultimately learned. Between the puppets, which included the characters Phineas T. Bluster and Princess Summerfallwinterspring, the clown Clarabelle, and Buffalo Bob's hosting and interaction with the highly excitable peanuts, *Howdy* was a rowdy, exciting show. The peanut gallery was always packed. In fact, at the height of *Howdy Doody*'s popularity, someone at NBC calculated that if all the children on the waiting list for the peanut gallery stood on line waiting to get in, those at the tail of the line would have finished college before their turn came.

In 1950, NBC acquired fifty Hopalong Cassidy movies starring Bill Boyd, made in the 1930s. They, too, were a big hit. For a long time, Howdy and Hoppy were the star entertainers for children. That same year the inventive WMAQ-TV in Chicago provided the network with another winner, *Zoo Parade*, from the city's Lincoln Park Zoo. The curator, a mild-mannered fellow, did show-and-tell numbers on myriad creatures in a very appealing way. His name was Marlin Perkins—now of *Wild Kingdom* fame.

The same station had a second captivating offering several years later, the mesmerizing *Ding Dong School* for preschoolers, conducted by the gentle "Miss Frances." Miss Frances simply sat on a stool, talked to children, and

Opposite: The Howdy Doody Show *was by far the most popular children's program of its time. It featured Clarabelle the clown, Howdy Doody, and Buffalo Bob Smith. During the 1970s, Buffalo Bob's popularity was still strong enough for him to make a national personal appearance tour. Left: The Horn & Hardart Children's Hour, starring Ed Herlihy. Below:* The Walter Williams Show *with Larry Semon had a makeshift set and an occasional scared child guest.*

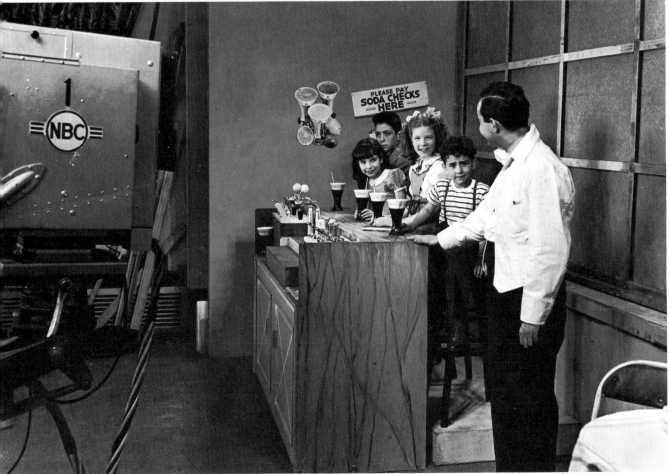

gave simple demonstrations of how to make things. On one occasion Miss Frances inadvertently created a shortage of pipe cleaners by showing children how to make animals out of them. Another show, featuring a cowboy act for children by a character known as "Cactus Jim" (who was Clarence Hartzell, the actor who played Uncle Fletcher in the old *Vic and Sade* radio show), started out with an inauspicious budget of forty dollars. But a year later it was more popular in the Chicago area than New York's network extravaganza, *Your Show of Shows.*

Kukla, Fran and Ollie, another WMAQ origination, became a long-time network favorite and in 1976 was back on the air again for NBC. Burr Tillstrom manipulates the puppets from backstage and Fran Allison, out front, has conversations with them. The show is never completely scripted because, as Tillstrom explains, "If I ever plotted exactly what I was going to say or do, Kukla and Ollie wouldn't work for me. They don't like cut-and-dried stuff. Fran wouldn't be able to talk to them, either."

Another early program, with quite a different format, was *Mr. Wizard.* The setting was a chemistry laboratory. At the beginning of each program Mr. Wizard had scientific equipment set up to do several experiments, and he also had on hand several youthful "assistants." The experiments were designed to answer questions that would interest young people.

In the late fifties and early sixties, it became clear that children were logging an astounding number of hours watching TV. Many people, including citizens and government groups and network executives as well, became increasingly concerned as to what effects, if any, all this TV watching was having on the minds of the young.

Cartoons, which had grown up as movie shorts, had come to TV—to all three networks. One typical offering was *Spider Man.* Another was the *Fantastic Four,* a group of superheroes (superheroes were big in those days). Still another was *Voyage to the Bottom of the Sea,* which seemed to feature a supermonster of the week. There were also the usual reruns of *Popeye, Bugs Bunny,* and *Roadrunner,* for years famous cartoons.

But no one knew much, if anything, about how one or another type of TV program actually affected children, or in what way, or whether violence as seen on television (in cartoon form or otherwise) instilled more aggression in children than they would otherwise have. In recent years, however, a number of in-depth sociological studies have been done to explore this issue. One of the most extensive (six volumes plus a summary) was carried out by the United States Surgeon General's office, which is concerned with matters affecting national physical and mental health (its most celebrated report linked cigarette smoking to lung cancer). Prior to the study, Senator Pastore of Rhode Island had held extensive hearings on the question. And after the report was released, he called another round to explore its findings.

Any solid investigation of any area of child psychology and behavior is frightfully complex—particularly if the subject is new and largely uninvestigated. For example: if a child chooses a particularly violent show and then acts aggressively toward other people, did the program provoke this behavior? Or did the child pick the show because he was aggressive to begin with? The Surgeon General's findings included indications that there might just be a connection between TV violence and aggressive behavior, though

Clockwise from above: Miss Frances, from Ding Dong School.
The gentlewoman (Dr. Frances Horwich) talked to
children and gave simple demonstrations of how to make
things; Burr Tillstrom brought his puppets, Kukla and Ollie,
to NBC from WMAQ in Chicago; MAQ also provided a show
from Chicago's Lincoln Park Zoo, called Zoo Parade, hosted
by the zoo's curator, Marlin Perkins, who later hosted Wild
Kingdom; in 1950 NBC acquired fifty Hopalong Cassidy movies,
which had been filmed in the 30s and starred William Boyd.

the relationships were far from clear. This being the case, virtually everyone at the hearings, including representatives from all three networks, concluded there was cause for concern and that more detailed studies were needed.

The Surgeon General's report had identified as one of the most desirable types of future research what the social scientists call a "longitudinal" study—one that observes the same group of people over an extended period of time. That matched the thinking at NBC, whose research department already had under way a study involving several hundred young boys, tracking their viewing habits and their behavior over three years. The extensive, detailed data are being analyzed now.

In the meantime, much of what had been, and was being aired for children was interesting as well as sophisticated. This was particularly true of children's specials. *Mr. Magoo's Christmas Carol* (1962) went both to repeats and reincarnations. So did *Charlie Brown's Christmas* (1964). Beginning with *Flipper* and *The Wonderful World of Disney* and later with *Wild Kingdom,* children were presented with amazing, intimate, and well-photographed explorations of the natural world.

Still, something had to be done to improve the Saturday morning schedule, and to this need the producers responded with both imagination and ingenuity. One innovative move was away from cartoons to live action programs. These make up nearly half of NBC's Saturday morning fare today. *Run, Joe, Run,* a juvenile version of *The Fugitive,* was about a nice but continually badmouthed German shepherd, always on the lam. *Land of the Lost* represented a breakthrough in special effects, combining live people and

Clockwise from below: Mickey Rooney stars in a children's special, Pinocchio; *Jonathan Winters is featured in a 1960* Shirley Temple Playhouse *production of* Babes in Toyland; *the popular Mr. Wizard, née Don Herbert, conducted his show from a chemistry laboratory, where he experimented with youthful "assistants"; a perennial cartoon favorite, Mr. Magoo, portrays Dickens's* Scrooge.

a primitive landscape with animated dinosaurs. It is still NBC's highest rated Saturday program. *Sigmund the Sea Monster* was a monster show, but with a difference. Sigmund couldn't hack it as a monster so two boys took him home and kept him in their clubhouse. *H. R. Puff 'n' Stuff* was still another "reverse" monster.

NBC has also produced nonviolent animations. *The Jetsons* came on as a very funny, hep, space-age version of the *Flintstones*. And a solid juvenile prime-time favorite, *Emergency*, was also produced in animation as *Emergency Plus 4*, the "plus 4" being four kids who accompanied the paramedics on their rounds. Another big revival was a twenty-six-week animated *Star Trek*, using the original writers and story editor. Still another of NBC's animated hits was the *Pink Panther Show.*

NBC has obviously demonstrated concern about what goes on the air for children, but the mere existence of concern does not tell any network much that is specifically useful in thinking about children's shows. So NBC established a Social Science Advisory Panel to explore the question in more detail, via promising new lines of research. One of the problems with child psychology, in terms of the effect of television, is that what one might think of as being sensible, or true, isn't necessarily that way at all. Recently NBC's Social Science group formulated a set of tentative criteria, based on their collective scientific training and knowledge of child psychology, and applied them to some children's shows.

CBS's much-maligned *Roadrunner* came up with a pretty good rating on several counts. For one thing, the plot is consistent. The coyote is always the "heavy," plotting one

Three of the newer entries in today's non-violence-oriented childrens shows: cartoon favorite the Pink Panther *(top right); the neighborhood friends of Bill Cosby's creation, Fat Albert (right);* Go-USA *(opposite) was a special bi-centennial series based on historical events during the Revolution in which young people played a significant part.*

146

or another kind of scheme to get the bird. But his plots always backfire. So the program teaches a good social lesson: violence is no solution to anything and "them that plots it get theirs in the end."

If the social behavior of young Americans seems to leave much to be desired, there are reasons for this that are far more profound than television. Until very recent times most people lived in a rather well-established social order of great stability, with a long-standing ethical fabric that held things together. Young people knew what was expected of them, had minimal options, and grew up to fit into the scheme of things and take their place in society. Now, however, especially in the industrialized nations, the old values are coming unglued. With increasing knowledge of other life-styles, an incredible degree of mobility, a great migration to the anonymity of the big city and its suburbs, a rising level of permissiveness, promiscuity, crime, and divorce, all the old stabilizing institutions—the family, the church, the community, the state—appear to be on rocky ground. This leaves many families in a strange and often frighteningly isolated position, feeling the traditional values that held things together slipping away.

The difficulties are compounded for American children because they live in the most media-laden country on earth, what with three TV networks, local stations, movies, all sorts of audiovisual materials in school, and so on. Their heads get crammed with information: about dinosaurs, space, wildlife, ecology, volcanoes, oceans—the list is endless. Are they having difficulty sorting it all out and making value judgments as to what is important and what is trivial, what it means, where they fit in, what they might become, what is expected of them?

Schools are aware of this and have introduced courses and seminars for young people to help them come to grips with some of these very basic human problems. Networks are aware, also. NBC introduced a special Bicentennial series, *Go-USA,* half-hour dramas aired on Saturdays and based on historical events during the American Revolution in which young people played key roles. The concept of *Go-USA* was to show children today that in 1776 young people had the same concerns they do now: Who am I? When am I afraid? When am I not afraid? Where will I go? How strong will I be? What are my inner resources? Will I come through in a pinch? Where do I fit in the world? Each of the programs showed young people confronted with difficult obstacles to overcome and tasks to perform, and how they struggled, often faltered, but finally came through.

Another NBC effort in special children's programming relates to the fact that most children go to school only because they have to, and often find the work dry and irrelevant to their immediate needs or interests. The network's *Special Treat* series dramatized such subjects as Einstein's theory of relativity, ways in which human beings meet the challenge of fear, and the universal language of music. For many of its shows NBC provides teacher's guides that list supplemental films, reading matter, and discussion and project possibilities for classroom use.

Still a third NBC series, *Take a Giant Step,* was produced by young people themselves. They invented situations that called for value judgments and filmed their own stories to dramatize the problem: whether it is right for people to steal if their families need their support, for example. The dramatizations were followed by panel discussions held by a group of young people; and for adults, there were some surprising observations.

The fact remains that one of television's worthiest purposes is one of the hardest to achieve. No responsible person can deny that television has a great capacity for educating young people and for enriching their lives. It can do this, however, only if it can engage and hold their attention. Combining and meeting these demands continues to challenge the networks, and while they have had some notable successes, they have also seen a great many noble attempts end in disappointment—not unlike parents, schools, and churches, which have been trying to reach children for centuries.

Tune in Tomorrow

Soap Operas and Quiz Shows

n the late 1960s, the women's movement began to be influential in America. A great many housewives were responding by hiring baby-sitters, full-time or part-time, to take care of their children while they went off to seek careers. Not all women, by any means, believed an outside career was the most rewarding approach. One who did not was Bryna P. Laub, a Massachusetts housewife and former high-school teacher whose husband Bernard is an aerospace project manager. The Laubs had just had a baby boy, and Bryna felt it was important for the child to have its mother at home. Moreover, she wanted to maintain her "habit"—she had been hopelessly hooked on television, particularly the soaps. Hers is an addiction that is surprisingly widespread among recent college graduates. The Laubs had TV sets located about their home so that Bryna could go about her housework and at the same time watch the daytime dramas on all three networks. Bryna became the local source of information on the latest plot developments. Since she watched every soap every day, her reputation spread. Strangers began to call for updates. Bernard suggested that maybe his wife ought to charge people for

her summaries. Why not turn all that TV time to profit by publishing a monthly newsletter that reviewed the plots of all the soaps that month—and offer it for sale?

So was born a modest publication called the *Daytime Serial Newsletter* (Bryna P. Laub, Publisher and Editor). Volume 1, Number 1, appeared in January, 1973, and the newsletter's availability, at $7.50 a year, was announced in one-inch ads in broadcasting magazines. The early issues consisted of eight to ten typewritten pages, single-spaced on both sides, folded once, and stapled for mailing.

Newsletter has undergone several transformations. Aside from plot summaries, it began to include other items of interest to daytime fans: cast changes, new shows and cancellations, announcements of books, records, Emmy nominations, and awards relating to the daytime serials. By 1974, the typeface was clearer, and some black-and-white photographs were being used. The following year, it was using two colors, as well as a better grade of paper. Now it is typeset and features a full-color cover.

Bryna Laub feels her newsletter should reflect the feeling of each show, especially the characters' interactions. That is what soap opera fans get hooked on. No bare script can convey the actual feeling of a show. A random sample from her newsletter (part of an episode from NBC's *The Doctors* in 1975) will suggest the kind of style she evolved:

Carolee Aldrich visits Baldwin College just in time to prevent the vulnerable Stacy Wells, Dr. Steve Aldrich's step-niece, from taking an overdose of sleeping pills. Warm-hearted Carolee wins the confidence of the troubled student and learns her art teacher, Peter Terrell, beguiled and deceived the innocent girl, until he was finally exposed by his long-suffering, but devoted wife, Linda, who had been through these little flings with her errant husband many times before.

Daytime dramas, particularly those that have gone to a full-hour format, are complex mosaics. As the plot gradually unfolds, incidents that seemed minor when they occurred, turn out, weeks or even months later, to have been of great significance. It is very easy to miss something important. A great many *Newsletter* subscribers are women who are away from home as little as one day a week. Thanks to the new periodical, they can easily catch up on any small but crucial episode missed.

The success of the *Daytime Serial Newsletter* indicates how important this form of entertainment has become across the nation. Whereas the term "soap opera" was once applied with an air of contempt, today it is more likely to express affection for a type of entertainment that is acceptable in almost every stratum of American society.

Soaps began in radio days. During the depression of the thirties, they provided escapism and humor for a nation in which nearly everyone was broke or close to it, immobilized, and frequently out of work. Audiences back then were primarily cooped-up blue-collar housewives and the elderly. The vast majority of today's audience is women, though more and more men are tuning in. It also includes the traditional retired people as well as students and the unemployed. But now the audience—which numbers more than a whopping 20 million—is no longer dominated by blue-collar housewives. This is largely because of the proliferation of the middle class in recent decades. This new majority falls into the eighteen to forty-nine age group and represents the heaviest buying power in America. Programming has changed accordingly. Most of the characters and situations in daytime drama today are middle- and even upper-class, though a few poor people and minority representatives appear on some of the shows. As a result of these developments, the daytime serials have become one of television's richest markets, attracting a host of advertisers to compete in the new and lucrative marketplace.

When it all began, no one had quite that kind of success story in mind, even in the plots of the soaps themselves. That was back in the mid twenties, on local radio stations only, and strictly in the evening. Daytime programming was nonexistent until the early 1930s. One of the major radio stations was WLW, owned by the Crosley Radio Corporation. In his comprehensive book *The Serials*, Raymond William Stedman observes that "the daytime offerings of WLW, Cincinnati, in the late fall of 1931, included *Beautiful Thoughts, Live Stock Reports, Our Daily Food, The Premium Man, Mrs. A. M. Goudiss* (what treasures did she unfold?), *Mouth Hygiene,* and *Edna Wallace Hopper.*" He goes on to

Radio soap forerunners, clockwise from above: Life Can Be Beautiful, *with Ralph Locke, John Holbrook, Alice Reinheart;* Against the Storm, *with Olive Deering, Chester Stratton;* When a Girl Marries, *which starred John Raby and Mary Jane Higby.*

observe that this was typical of programming for women in those days.

The idea of serials, or drama, on the installment plan was certainly not new. Charles Dickens and Feodor Dostoevski were published in serial. In the days of silent movies, *The Perils of Pauline* and *The Adventures of Tarzan* were tremendously popular. In Chicago, in 1925, a young vaudeville team, Marian and Jim Jordan, introduced a weekly evening show on WENR called *The Smith Family.* It contained many of the ingredients that would later characterize soap operas. Later, the Jordans became known to the country as *Fibber McGee and Molly.* Another Chicago taproot of the soaps was apparently *Sam 'n' Henry* on WGN in 1926, the creation of Charles Correll and Freeman Gosden. This show became a national rage in a few short years as *Amos 'n' Andy.* It, too, had a built-in tune-in value. It was aired five nights a week, as a fifteen-minute program (the basic time span for such shows in the early days).

Other early shows, though still in fifteen-minute evening time slots, reflected more directly what was to come. In 1931, NBC brought to the network *The Rise of the Goldbergs,* which had proved a hit on the New York local station, WJZ, and that same year presented a droll trio of women friends, *Clara, Lu, 'n' Em.* A year earlier in Chicago, a show called *Painted Dreams* had become the first daytime serial. *Painted Dreams* introduced an element that was to become the hallmark of all the soaps to follow: intertwined lives and a number of parallel plots. From this credo author Irna Phillips was later to create three of the most durable TV daytime dramas of all: *As the World Turns, Another World,* and *The Guiding Light,* all of which are still running.

As everyone knows, daytime drama came to be known as soap opera because the manufacturers of soap products were the dominant sponsors (which was logical, consider-

ing the audience was predominantly housewives). When Pepsodent toothpaste decided to take a flier on network radio by sponsoring *Amos 'n' Andy,* no one knew quite what results to expect. But when the program skyrocketed into a national pastime, a gratified Pepsodent sales department quickly acquired *The Goldbergs* as a backup. Colgate followed suit in 1932, picking up *Clara.* In 1933 a bellwether for the future was sounded. Procter & Gamble came on the NBC network with what was to prove one of the all-time radio hits: *Oxydol's Own Ma Perkins.*

By the late 1930s, a variety of fifteen-minute daytime serials was flourishing on the air. They proved to be a tremendous business success for the sponsors and contributed a great deal to the increasing power of network radio. The actors clustered around a single microphone, scripts in hand, and projected with considerable realism the day's moment of drama. Usually they were supported by an organist, who was skillful enough to provide a large variety of background moods: suspense, a feeling of unrequited love, a sense of the ominous, a touch of joy.

A partial list of soap opera "graduates" is impressive: Orson Welles, Macdonald Carey, Van Heflin, Agnes Moorehead, Mercedes McCambridge, Jeanette Nolan, Art Carney, Gary Merrill, Paul Ford, Anne Francis, Richard Widmark.

When it became clear that television was the coming medium, the question of how to transplant the unseen, imaginary world of daytime radio into the visible world of TV became of some concern. Many attempts were made, but only CBS's *The Guiding Light* survived the transplant—and is still very much alive and well. The previous year, CBS had introduced two original shows for television that are still going strong: *Search for Tomorrow* and *Love of Life.* And in 1956, CBS made an innovative move, amid much doubt and

head-wagging. It broke the traditional fifteen-minute format and introduced two new half-hour serials. One was *As the World Turns* (Irna Phillips again); the other was *The Edge of Night* (now on ABC).

Meanwhile, the daytime drama efforts of NBC and ABC did not fare very well. But both networks finally scored in 1963, the former with *The Doctors* and the latter with *General Hospital.*

The following year, NBC added *Another World* and then, in 1965, came *Days of Our Lives*—the creation of another grand dame of serial drama, Betty Corday, who developed *Days* with her late husband Ted. Three years later, NBC spun *Somerset* out of *Another World.* In 1975, NBC took its two most popular soaps, *Another World* and *Days of Our Lives,* to a full-hour format.

What is so fascinating about these big daytime serials to so many people? Raymond Stedman, clearly a serious student of the genre, answers the question this way:

> The daytime serial, today as in the radio era, benefits from a cumulative factor. With each episode watched, the viewer invests more deeply in the undertaking. The continuing characters, expanded by the illusion of reality that accompanies the extended action, become as real as neighbors. More real, perhaps, because the viewer knows every secret—the child a mother cannot acknowledge, the disease that will destroy a young surgeon's sight, the marriage that is in name only. This detailed knowledge adds nuance to each piece of action, and it adds meaning that critics (who watch only occasionally, and clinically) cannot detect or appraise. Those who do not follow a particular serial regularly are like those who enter a church during a rainstorm and witness a wedding. They see what takes place, but not through the

eyes of the bride's mother or family doctor or disappointed suitor.

Aristotelian tragedy it ain't. Tragedy of that dimension calls for epic characters. But character, in a lesser sense, is the hinge on which all the successful soaps turn. That is what all writers of daytime drama strive for; along with interaction among the characters. A good, old-fashioned Gothic dynasty is a perfect vehicle for family secrets and mysteries, as well as closeted skeletons. The Hortons of *Days of Our Lives,* where Macdonald Carey plays the patriarch, Dr. Tom Horton, are into four generations now. Interaction is one reason so many of the characters in the serials are professionals, usually doctors or lawyers, sometimes architects and contractors. Hospitals provide a natural setting for bringing together all kinds of people and problems. By the same token, a good courtroom drama is hard to beat.

In the soaps, everyone's love life is messed up in one way or another. For the most part, characters move about as though each is under his or her own special cloud. It cannot be otherwise. Viewers are continually writing in to ask why one or another character cannot be happy, why two star-crossed lovers cannot be united. Happiness, however, is not a staple of drama in any medium, and as soon as it rears its ugly head viewer interest is apt to fall off.

If, in the serials, the characters seem not too well attuned to their fates, this only raises the level of audience interest. The odds are very good that "we" will be let in on what is really going on, even if those in the drama are unaware of it. Viewers want to shout: "Hey! Watch out!" This sense of participation, coupled with anticipation, is heightened by the way the soaps are done. Actors use pauses to increase the effect of the drama in progress. In actual

Left to right: Stars of Days of Our Lives *MacDonald Carey and Frances Reid, 1965; also from* Days of Our Lives *John Lupton and Regina Gleason, 1968; a 1964 picture of Leon Janney and Virginia Dwyer of* Another World.

153

scripts, this is written in as a "beat," to indicate a pause to heighten significance and dramatic effect. Here is an example from the script for episode 2,596 from *Days*:

ADELE
Oh, Brooke. I'm so sorry.
BROOKE
(GENTLY)
That you took a drink of wine, Mama?
(BEAT)
Or that I saw you take it?

As in the radio soaps, this attenuated effect is heightened by music and enhanced by the slow fade-out on a significant thought or development.

Sometimes, viewers identify too completely with the soaps. Actresses who have played bitches on the screen and actors who have played heels have been assaulted in department stores and supermarkets by irate TV viewers wielding handbags.

The nighttime drama are necessarily episodic and are typically wrapped up in an hour. But in the soaps, a character may suffer the consequences of an act for weeks, months, years, and (to date), as long as a quarter century. Suffering is what keeps the soaps going.

When, in 1964, ABC came up with its sensationalized nighttime soap, *Peyton Place*, people thought TV "had gone about as far as it could go." Not so. Since then, daytime drama has tackled, usually with some understanding and illumination, such subjects as nymphomania, abortion, homosexuality, frigidity, impotence, incest, miscegenation, drug addiction, venereal disease, seduction, alcoholism, childbirth, child abuse, mastectomy, amnesia, insanity, the Vietnam war, cervical cancer, racism, artificial insemination, miscarriage, hysterectomy, and illegitimacy. Many writers of daytime drama shows take a quiet pride in presenting some of these difficult subjects with taste and intelligence. They are also proud of their contribution toward liberating women from the stereotyped housewife role, by showing them on the air performing competently as lawyers, doctors, and other professionals.

Establishing a successful daytime television serial is a gamble. The show comes on cold, committed to being on the air five days a week. It must be on at least a year before anyone can begin to consider whether it has a chance of success. It takes that long for it to build a loyal following (or fail to). The interwoven characters, plots, and subplots take time to develop. You really have to settle in with a soap and give it time.

Typically, the head writer of a soap produces what is known in the trade as "the bible," a narrative of well over a hundred pages that projects the basic story over the coming year. He or she then breaks the bible down into chapter and verse, outlining the progress of the story on a day-to-day basis in terms of the six episodes each day's hour show comprises. The head writer supervises the work of staff writ-

154

Above: From Somerset, *Barry Jenner and Fawne Harriman as Tony and Ginger Cooper, and Gary Swanson and Susan McDonald as Greg Mercer and Jill Grant. Opposite: 1966 stars from* Another World, *Colgate Salsbury and Gaye Huston.*

ers, as many as six or more, who create the dialogue. Then the whole show is edited by its top writers for continuity, dramatic progression, sense, sensibility, and suspense.

Though it may appear that a year's worth of serial is then set, this is not at all the case. The public's response to the unfolding drama is continually monitored. If a particular character or subplot seems to be dragging, it can be quietly written out of the show. If a competing program seems to have a particularly hot episode going in its favor, the writers will huddle to see how their own product might be beefed up. Now and then, a minor character is introduced. Though it may appear that he just dropped in to fix the sink, he may have considerable audience appeal. In that case, he becomes a part of the plot, possibly bringing his own family and perhaps community or hometown aboard. All in all, the soaps are as subject to the vicissitudes of fate as are their characters.

Taping such a show five days a week, several weeks before air time, involves a grueling workday, beginning at 6:00 A.M. and ending at 5:00 P.M. or a bit earlier if all goes well. The producer and director for the day are on the scene promptly, as are their assistants and the production crew. The actors and actresses appear somewhat later, depending on where their sequences fall in the show. They have to be very professional during the long day of rehearsals. When air time comes, a character who was in Act II has to remember what has transpired and has to determine how he or she should be psychologically by Act IV or V. If a particu-

lar subplot becomes hot, an actor or actress may have to be on the set day after day, which can be exhausting. On the other hand, the leisure that comes when a subplot grows dormant can cause a performer to worry about his future with the show. Some actors and actresses who have been through the rigors of soaps and survived include: Jack Lemmon, Eva Marie Saint, Tony Randall, Efrem Zimbalist, Jr., Sandy Dennis, Dyan Cannon, Hal Holbrook, Jill Clayburgh, Ellen Burstyn, Donna Mills, Bonnie Bedelia, Patrick O'Neal, Lois Nettleton, Lee Grant, Jessica Walters, and Trish Van Devere.

In the production of a typical current hour show, the first part of the early morning is devoted to a dry run, in which the acts are blocked out. Then there is a technical meeting on the day's production. After lunch comes a brief meeting about technical production problems, and then comes the dress rehearsal. A good producer helps to shape a scene in dramatic terms. In effect, he or she acts as another pair of eyes for the director, who is so involved technically that he cannot detect every dramatic nuance. During the blocking, the producer may also note little slip-ups (a badly composed picture or an excessive highlight on a large prop) for correction before the show is finally taped—which is done in sequence, from the Prologue through Act VI, almost as if the show were on the air live.

By dress rehearsal time, the whole focus of the program centers on the director, who is seated at a big console in the control booth, flanked by the control room staff. Before him

Early quiz shows were zany as well as diverse. Clockwise from below: 1940 Quiz Kids with Joan Irene Bishop, Gerard Darrow, and Charles Schwartz; host Ralph Edwards and Marie McLean enjoy a good sidesplitter on Truth or Consequences in 1941; Groucho Marx with one of his typical contestants on You Bet Your Life; Information Please had radio editor Alton Cook, journalists John Kiernan, Alice Miller, F. P. Adams, and Clifton Fadiman as the show's moderator.

is an array of monitors. The central one shows him the scene as it will actually be taped. Beside this are other monitors, which show what each camera on the stage is "seeing." Usually two cameras are used for a given scene, though more may be required if the set is complex. In a simple scene—two people having coffee in a kitchen, for instance—camera # 1 may be set for a medium long shot showing part of the kitchen and the two people together. Camera # 2 might be set for a close-up of the person who will speak first. So the scene may open with a fade-in on Camera # 1, establishing the location and the people. Then there might be a cut to Camera # 2 as the first person begins speaking. Meanwhile, Camera # 1 would have zoomed in for a tight shot of the second person, so that when this actor picks up the conversation there will be a close-up of him or her. Each short act in the show is broken down into perhaps several dozen different shots, which are numbered sequentially in the director's script. So as the scene progresses, he cuts

Above: Jack Bailey crowns a new queen on Queen for a Day,
a woman whose story was deemed most tragic by the
studio audience. Opposite: Quiz master Bert Parks watches
a contestant Break the Bank on the 1950 NBC show.

back and forth from one camera to the other, following the action.

During dress rehearsal, and especially during actual taping, the director "flies" the show, like a pilot in control of an airplane. He knows the script by heart, follows all the cues, and directs the camera switches. Each time he does this, the technical director pushes a button, cutting from one camera to another. The image of the camera that is being taped appears on the main monitor as well as on the camera's own monitor. The director understands his characters' relationships and the essential pacing of the show. In setting up each episode, he determines the camera angles and positions that will make the most of the atmosphere in each scene. And when the final taping comes, he almost literally lives with what is happening on the main monitor, cueing cameras and bringing in music or superimposed flashbacks or bits of earlier conversations that a character may be remembering. To do this he has to be in good shape physically, rested, and emotionally up, for the whole process is exhausting. This is why, on a big show like *Days of Our Lives,* there are four directors and none works more than twice a week. Otherwise, when the faithful "tune in tomorrow for another full hour of drama," there might be nothing on the air but soap suds.

For years, quiz shows were an innocent staple of radio programming. Out of Chicago and onto CBS came the *Quiz Kids,* a favorite program during the forties that pitted a cluster of amazingly erudite youngsters against questions too tough for the average adult listener. Another favorite of the radio era was NBC's *Information Please,* which featured equally erudite adults, among them Clifton Fadiman; the eccentric and iconoclastic concert pianist Oscar Levant; and John Kiernan, a master of sports and the natural world.

They were fed every conceivable kind of question, including occasional music-identification ones that Oscar answered at the piano. Their collective fund of miscellaneous knowledge was stupefying. Ralph Edwards's *Truth or Consequences* was one of the few game shows to make it from radio to television. It proved equally viable when made visible because the "consequences" suffered by many a contestant could be counted on to yield funny sight gags.

In 1950, Groucho Marx came on with his hilarious quiz show, *You Bet Your Life.* The show was done on film on the West Coast and shipped to New York for airing. (At that time, there was no coast-to-coast coaxial cable for transmitting live programs.) One of the hallmarks of Groucho's show was the selection of amusing and incongruous couples who appeared as contestants. This was no accident. The writers of the show had a talent scout on the road for weeks on end. The material that the writers prepared for Groucho concerned specific individuals and, more often than not, it evoked his ad-lib remarks. Some of the exchanges were memorable. On one occasion, the following occurred with a clergyman:

Groucho: Tell me. I understand that men of the cloth are not of great means. How can you afford a vacation here on the West Coast?
Clergyman: Well, Groucho, I just had a windfall.
Groucho (arching his bushy eyebrows insinuatingly): Oh? Have you tried Alka Seltzer?

A year earlier, in 1949, the tone of quiz shows had changed forever. ABC put a program on the air at prime time called *Stop the Music.* It featured the orchestra of Harry Salter, and Bert Parks was the host-announcer. The orchestra would play a hit tune, during which Parks would suddenly cry out: "Stop the music!" At that point, Parks would

Two of the more well-known winners of the $64,000 Question, the show that rocked the industry when it was revealed that some contestants had been given the answers beforehand, unbeknownst to the network. Dr. Joyce Brothers (top) won $64,000 for her endlessly thorough knowledge of boxing, and Bronx shoemaker Geno Prato won a like amount for his ability to answer questions on opera. Opposite: Hosts Alex Trebek and Ruta Lee oversee NBC's High Rollers.

make a telephone call to some randomly selected individual anywhere in the country. If the person answered, he would ask: "Are you listening?" If so, then Parks, his voice rising in excitement and suspense, would ask: "Can you identify the tune?" And if the listener could name the tune, then WOW! That person was in line for gifts worth thousands of dollars. It was terribly exciting, the granddaddy of the shows of today that have contestants who scream, jump up and down, and occasionally faint. Stop the Music killed Fred Allen's nighttime NBC show dead. Naturally, it quickly spawned other big giveaway imitations like Shoot the Moon, Hit the Jackpot, and Chance of a Lifetime. Big bonanza shows of this type quickly sprouted on television in the following years, notably Tic Tac Dough, The $64,000 Question, Twenty-one, and The Big Surprise. They presented quite a contrast to the modest gleanings on Groucho Marx's You Bet Your Life. Now the winnings were no longer merchandise, but hard cash, and lots of it. All sorts of supposedly "little people"—teachers, ministers, cobblers, storekeepers—miraculously guessed correct answers and struck it rich, often to the tune of $100,000 or more. The public loved it and the contestants became brief folk heroes. One of the winners, a legacy of the giveaways, was Dr. Joyce Brothers. She had a photographic memory and could "microfilm" in her head vast quantities of information about anything (in this case boxing and boxers).

But then, in the summer of 1959, it all came crashing down. Ugly rumors had been floating around New York for months. Then the Colgate-Palmolive Company abruptly cancelled its show Dotto. Other cancellations followed. The cancellations were followed by a series of recantations. A parade of former money-winners from numerous quiz shows owned up to the fact that the producers had given them the answers beforehand, and that their anguished, tormented faces on the air, as they presumably struggled for the correct response, had been nothing but an act. The biggest loser of all the big winners, in terms of prestige, was Charles Van Doren of the prestigious Van Doren literary family. He had been riding high on Twenty-One, locked into a struggle for the really big marbles with Herbert Stempel. It was a dramatic confrontation while it lasted. And it held viewers spellbound for weeks. Which is why the producers had rigged the show to begin with. Ultimately, Van Doren ended up with $129,000 in winnings plus a $50,000 job with NBC as a history consultant (which proved, in passing, that the network had been just as gulled by the goings on as had its viewers). But with the crash, all that evaporated (including Van Doren's job). Many contestants, including a hapless Charles Van Doren, and many producers maintained their innocence. But when the whole question came under Congressional scrutiny, Charles Van Doren and others confessed to the sham at a hushed Congressional hearing in Washington, D.C. Yet he and the other contestants were more deceived than deceiving, for the producers had convinced them the whole charade was just a game, a new kind of magic show. Congress could hardly resist conjuring up the Van Doren name in the course of its incantations. So Charles Van Doren, no more venal than most Americans when faced with the prospects of such an easy hustle, and certainly less so than the producers who hustled him, became the fall guy of record in the whole sorry mess.

The game show scandals were compounded by the "payola" scandals, which erupted about the same time. It was revealed that executives of various recording compa-

Today's soap operas are not only sophisticated in their choice of subject matter, but are taped with great care and professionalism. Sets, while not elaborate, are nonetheless expensive and authentic-looking. The actors are serious; no longer is playing the soaps considered a second-rate acting job. Clockwise from left: View from above of Burbank Studio 9, control room, and set from Days of Our Lives.

Opposite: The cast from How to Survive a Marriage, *which was one of the more frank soap operas; nurses from* The Doctors *enjoy the company of guest Don Imus, who made his fame from New York's NBC radio show,* Imus in the Morning; *MacDonald Carey and Frances Reid.*

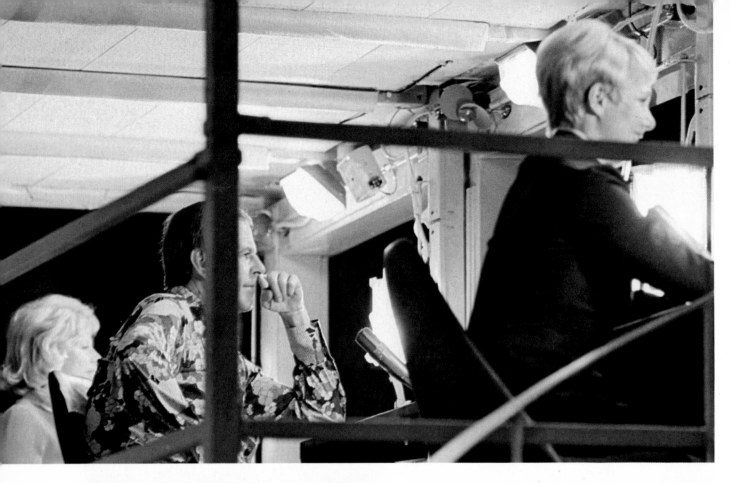

KAREN VALENTINE

Nine stars, host Peter Marshall, two contestants, rich prizes, and a barrel of one-liners have made the Hollywood Squares *TV's most popular quiz show. It is seen daily, Monday through Friday, as well as twice weekly in the evening. First prize is a car, but the success of the show rests with its rotating list of stars, the favorite of whom is Paul Lynde (top).*

Clockwise from above: Art Fleming hosts Jeopardy, a long-running quiz show whose strength was the difficulty of the questions; Bill Cullen asks the questions on Three on a Match; Charles Van Doren (left), the most famous of all $64,000 Question winners, was defeated on Twenty-One. He missed the name of the king of Belgium. Bill Mazer and Reach for the Stars.

nies had been giving money and other gifts under the table to various disc jockeys around the country to get the DJs to plug their records. Not only had the public, which had accepted the game shows in good faith and was avidly rooting for one or another participant, been totally deceived, it was also outraged. So were the federal government and assorted state governments. The feeling had become so intense that even President Eisenhower, a cautious and prudent man, had asked the Justice Department to look into the whole affair. Worse than that, for the networks anyway, was the fact that the American people were devastated by the scandals and had lost faith in the integrity of radio and television. The financial foundations of the media were built on advertising, which in turn depended on the public's belief that the claims and assertions of advertisers for their products were valid. The development of careful procedures to assure and maintain integrity was the upshot. And today there may be no area in the business or entertainment world that is so thoroughly policed as television's quiz and game shows. Each of the three networks has a department whose main responsibility is assuring the integrity of these programs. On NBC's *Hollywood Squares*, for instance, the stars in the squares are frequently given answers to questions, or at least hints as to the subject matter the questions will cover, so that they will be better prepared to come up with funny remarks if called upon—which is the real attraction of this particular program and the key element that audiences enjoy. Although this procedure has no effect whatever on how well any contestant will make out, NBC

nevertheless feels obliged to insert at the end of each program an explanation of what has been done.

The big giveaway shows were prime-time, evening shows. But after the bubble burst, NBC turned to daytime, with emphasis on the morning hours, creating a whole parade of milder and scrupulously honest programs. Ralph Edwards's old radio show, *Truth or Consequences*, had already made a successful TV debut in the mid fifties. Bob Barker hosted the new program on which contestants were entered into all sorts of silly contests. The show was such a hit it gave birth to *People Are Funny*. NBC, which early on had had a weak showing in daytime drama, fared much better with its daytime games, *It Could Be You, Queen for a Day*, and *Let's Make a Deal*.

By any standards *Queen for a Day* was an incredible show. Three women contestants would appear before the audience, each with a tale of woe. Their stories of misery and misfortune were tales of unremitting calamity. Here is an imaginary scenario that is, nevertheless, not the least exaggerated: "It wasn't so bad when my husband died, though it did turn out his life insurance was worthless. The salesman had been a fraud. But then my sister became bedridden with a mysterious illness, and it lasted for seven years. I sold off all the furniture and appliances, which kept things going for a few months. But the night before I was to sell the house it caught fire and burned to the ground. Our fire insurance was very small so I took John and Linda and we moved into my sister's house to consolidate things. One night Linda, who had always been sickly, developed these violent spasms and died before the doctor could get there. And several weeks after that . . ." And so it went. After all three contestants had presented their laments, the applause, registered on an "applause meter," from the audience determined whose story was the most doleful. Whereupon that "lucky lady" would become "queen for a day." The emcee, Jack Bailey, placed a crown on her head, an elegant robe around her shoulders, and she was showered with expensive gifts.

Though game shows today still offer some grand prizes, any and all winnings are scrupulously come by these days. The days when contestants were rigged to become public heroes are long dead. The packagers—independent producers that supply NBC's shows—pick people the audience can identify with. How that identification comes about is the key to what makes a successful game show for NBC. In almost all cases the viewer can play the game along with the contestants, and at about the same intellectual level. On *Concentration*, for example, as the contestants eliminate blocks, the resulting vacant spaces reveal parts of one of the show's features, a rebus. As more and more of the rebus is revealed, the contestants strain to guess what it means. So do viewers. Since the rebus always represents a familiar saying, such as "It's raining cats and dogs" or "A stitch in time saves nine," the audience is usually on an equal competitive footing with the players, and the viewer may at times guess the answer before the contestants do. Which is very satisfying, and also engrossing. The same applies to a show like *Wheel of Fortune*, in which panels are eliminated to reveal letters that spell something simple: "Prince Valiant," for example, or "Gunga Din."

Other shows involve gambling, a feature that is of interest to almost everyone. Such a show is *High Rollers*. And *The Hollywood Squares* is a hit for the very obvious reason that everyone loves to watch "the squares" come up with fast, one-line quips. To any veteran pinball-machine player, *The Magnificent Marble Machine* was very involving indeed, because one could play along with the players, vicariously "working" the machine to keep the big ball bouncing against the bumpers, maintaining it in play in the process.

Contestants are carefully screened for all the game shows, interviewed, and sometimes even put through trial runs of whatever game is involved. The producers have specifications for the kinds of people they want: what they are looking for are "smiling, happy, outgoing, and enthusiastic people." Apparently there are many, many such folk abroad in the land, because the waiting list for each show is quite long. Though the shows are aired each day, they are taped in advance; as many as ten episodes may be taped in the course of a single day. Thus a winning contestant who, on the air, "comes back the next day," in all likelihood will have come back after lunch. One special feature of taping the game shows involves the *Squares*. This show, unlike the others, is done on weekends, starting late in the afternoon and running close to midnight. The reason is that the celebrities are usually busy doing their own acts during the week.

One special feature of all NBC's game shows today is their imaginative and impressive sets, a far, far cry from the jerry-built setup Groucho used on *You Bet Your Life*. And what the viewer sees on the air is almost totally an illusion. In the flesh, backstage and not in actual use, the sets for *Squares, Wheel of Fortune*, and other game shows are mundane in appearance and quite unimpressive, though one easily recognizes them. Yet when they are "on," and carefully lit for effect, they are completely resplendent to the TV camera.

Truth or Consequences *(one of the few shows to make it from radio to television) starred Bob Barker and featured such homely happenings as the reunion of lost relatives. Here, a brother and sister are reunited after 30 years of being apart. The show obtained a visa for her from Poland.*

Fact, Fiction, or Pure Fantasy

Dramatic Specials

In the early years of television, the New York theatrical world, with its tradition of presenting both classic and contemporary drama, with its many fine actresses and actors, producers and directors, proved a gold mine for a variety of special dramatic TV programs. NBC, with its headquarters in the city, early became the acknowledged leader in mining this fertile vein. NBC has been aided by one advertiser, Hallmark Cards, which for a quarter century has sponsored some of the finest dramatic productions to be seen on television. The programs, over the years, have included both classic and contemporary plays, operas, and musical comedies. They have won more than thirty-five Emmy Awards. Hallmark's interest in underwriting this unique programming is straightforward. The corporation likes to associate quality with its name and the cards it offers. To celebrate its twenty-fifth anniversary on NBC, Hallmark is presenting (during the Christmas season) a special two-hour musical version of Sir James M. Barrie's timeless and delightful play, *Peter Pan,* starring Mia Farrow as the boy who refuses to grow up and Danny Kaye as the transparently sinister Captain Hook.

Not all NBC drama has been Hallmark-sponsored. Another long-term sponsor has been the American Telephone and Telegraph Company, which goes back to radio days with NBC, when the *Bell Telephone Hour* brought classical music to delighted homes all across the land. Currently, AT&T presents an occasional special on the *Bell System Family Theater.* A notable production was *Jane Eyre,* a

dramatization of Charlotte Brontë's brooding and suspenseful novel. It starred George C. Scott and Susannah York, with an all-British supporting cast including Jack Hawkins and Nyree Dawn Porter. *Jane Eyre* got rave reviews, was the most widely viewed dramatic special of the 1970-71 season, and was reprised the following year. On the occasion of the one-hundredth anniversary of the invention of the telephone by Alexander Graham Bell, AT&T celebrated itself in March, 1976, with the ninety-minute *Bell Telephone Jubilee,* hosted by Bing Crosby and Liza Minnelli.

Though occasionally one or another corporation is the sole sponsor of a special, more often than not there is multiple sponsorship. And a dramatic special may originate in many different ways. In 1956, under the aegis of a special NBC documentary group known as *Wide Wide World,* the network presented a three-hour color feature film, *Richard III,* starring Sir Laurence Olivier and Sir Ralph Richardson. The picture was made in England. Its TV debut was timed for the American release. Four years later, Hallmark introduced a new *Macbeth,* starring the famous Shakespearian actor Maurice Evans, with Judith Anderson playing the Scottish tyrant's conniving wife. The pair had done an earlier Hallmark *Macbeth* in 1954, but now there were significant differences. The new production was filmed in color. Further, it was shot on location in Scotland.

Dramatic specials aim for top performances, a dramatic script, and good location shooting. *Hans Brinker* was shot in Amsterdam; *Heidi* was filmed in Switzerland for a

Top: The first Broadway hit to be televised with its original cast was Susan and God *with Gertrude Lawrence, Paul McGrath, and Nancy Coleman. Opposite:* The Late Mr. Bean, *a special that starred Lillian Gish and Burt Lydell.*

Top: The use of theatrical motion pictures in network television was a relatively new idea in 1956, when NBC put on the air Richard III, starring Sir Laurence Olivier. The movie was shot in England. Above: The Colgate Theatre presents The Contest, a dramatic special starring Tom Ewell and Bill Lynn. Right: Blithe Spirit.

Top: Betty Hutton stars in a special television production of Satin and Spurs. *Opposite: Elizabeth Montgomery portrayed a woman raped in the dramatic and honest presentation of* A Case of Rape. *In the show, Montgomery presses charges against a rapist, but loses her husband in the process.*

backdrop of magnificent mountains and Alpine meadows; *Jane Eyre* was done on the bleak, desolate Yorkshire moors in England, where the story takes place. *The Count of Monte Cristo* was filmed in Italy, complete with an ancient stone seaside fortress that looks for all the world like the forbidding Chateau d'If, where Edmond Dantes was wrongfully imprisoned for fourteen years. Recreating such a set in the studio not only would be difficult; it would also be beyond the reach of TV drama budgets. A show like *Monte Cristo,* if done well, has a lot more going for it than mere realism. It is a corking good yarn. The show proved so popular that the network repeated it and was inspired to produce another great vintage masterpiece of the same type, *The Man in the Iron Mask*—which required scouting the whole of France to come up with locations for the great reception halls and interiors the story requires. The realism of Daniel Defoe's *Robinson Crusoe* was heightened by the fact that it was shot on an island: Tobago, in the West Indies. That particular show was produced for NBC by the British Broadcasting Corporation. (In recent years, NBC and the BBC have begun to work closely together, coproducing programs of mutual interest.)

Hallmark's *Teacher, Teacher* (1969) was an original drama about efforts to teach a mentally retarded youth. It won many awards, including an Emmy for the season's outstanding drama. It starred David McCallum, Ossie Davis, George Grizzard, and a retarded fourteen-year-old named Billy Schulman, who was the focus of the drama. Another Hallmark production, *A Storm in Summer* (1970), by Rod Serling, featured Peter Ustinov as a sad and elderly Jewish delicatessen owner in a small upstate New York town who became the unwilling summer host to a black youngster from Harlem. Ustinov won an Emmy, and so did the show. The following year Hallmark scored once more with Arthur Miller's play *The Price,* which starred George C. Scott (who won an Emmy), Barry Sullivan, and Colleen Dewhurst. More recently, NBC presented *The Entertainer,* based on English writer John Osborne's 1957 play about a British music-hall performer on the skids. In the play, Sir Laurence Olivier gave a brilliant performance as the shabby song-and-dance man, as he did in the British film version, which followed thereafter. For NBC, a British production group picked an American location, Santa Cruz, California, that housed a run-down amusement park and theater. And it chose a different time setting: 1944, toward the end of World War II. Jack Lemmon, who is not only a superb actor, but can sing, dance, and play the piano, found the role of the song-and-dance man irresistible and played it to perfection. Ray Bolger gave an equally great performance in the part of his show-business father.

A dramatic special can be based on fact, fiction, or pure fantasy. It can even be a solo act, if the performer is as painstaking and gifted as Hal Holbrook. His *Mark Twain Tonight* on CBS was a captivating performance, so real one felt the great American humorist had returned from the dead. Holbrook repeated that triumph with the special NBC Bicentennial series *Sandburg's Lincoln.* And Henry Fonda's *Clarence Darrow* on NBC demonstrated again the power of the solo performance when graced by the talents of a gifted actor.

In recent years the NBC-BBC relationship has intensified. With the coproduction of Arthur Miller's *After the Fall,* starring Faye Dunaway, Christopher Plummer, and Bibi Anderson, the two networks launched the beginning of a long-

176

Clockwise from left: Chrysler Theatre's Have Girls, Will Travel, *with Bob Hope and Jill St. John; Simon Ward as Major John André and Richard Basehart as George Washington in Hallmark's* Valley Forge; *William Holden in television's adaptation of Joseph Wambaugh's* The Blue Knight; *Hallmark's 1965 production of* The Magnificent Yankee, *featuring James Daly and Lynn Fontanne;* The Rivalry, *starring Charles Durning as Stephen Douglas and Arthur Hill as Abraham Lincoln.*

Above: Groucho Marx in The Mikado. *Opposite: Richard Chamberlain as Edmond Dantés and Taryn Power as Valentine deVillefort in* The Count of Monte Cristo.

Clockwise from left: James Stewart and Helen Hayes perform memorably in Harvey; *Kurt Yaghjian, boy soprano, as Amahl in Gian Carlo Menotti's Christmas opera,* Amahl and the Night Visitors, *which premiered in 1963; Martin Sheen awaits the firing squad in* The Execution of Private Slovik; *John Forsythe in* Teahouse of the August Moon.

Opposite: Richard Burton in a reflective moment as Winston
Churchill, in The Gathering Storm. Above: Cyrano,
starring José Ferrer, Christopher Plummer, and Claire Bloom.

term exchange of major dramatic specials. One two-hour Bicentennial special, *The Inventing of America,* about the impact of American inventions on the United States, is of interest to British viewers as well. A more recent agreement involves Sir Laurence Olivier, Granada Television of Britain, and NBC-TV. The trio will produce several TV plays a year by outstanding American dramatists: Eugene O'Neill, Tennessee Williams, Arthur Miller, Robert E. Sherwood, Lillian Hellman, George S. Kaufman, and others. Olivier will act as host and, occasionally, will perform in the series. By expanding its production capabilities in these and other cooperative directions, both NBC and its coproducers will be able to create more high-quality dramatic specials than ever before, and audiences in America, Europe, and elsewhere will be the beneficiaries.

Opposite top: The Lunts in The Magnificent Yankee.
Opposite bottom: Mary Martin and John Raitt from their Broadway production of Annie Get Your Gun.
Above: Burgess Meredith stars in Eli Whitney.

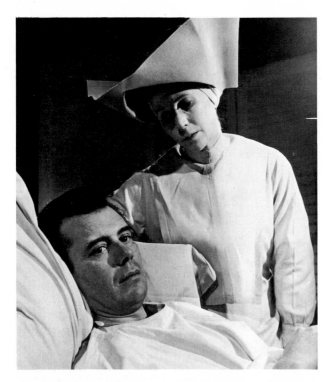

Clockwise from opposite: Julie Harris as Queen Victoria and James Donald as Prince Albert in Laurence Hausman's play Victoria Regina; Stanley Holloway, Ricardo Montalban, and Bert Lahr in the long-running off-Broadway play The Fantasticks; Dirk Bogarde and Julie Harris in Little Moon of Alban; Barry Sullivan and George C. Scott in Arthur Miller's powerful, award-winning drama The Price.

Clockwise from left: In 1960 Steven Hill and Martin Balsam starred in a two-part dramatic special, Sacco and Vanzetti; *Hallmark's 1965 production of* Inherit the Wind, *starring Melvyn Douglas as Henry Drummond and Doug Chapin as schoolboy Howard; Davis Roberts, Robert Hooks, Frederick O'Neal, and Claudia McNeil in* Frederick Douglass, *on* Profiles in Courage, *which portrayed the slave and abolitionist leader; Hal Holbrook in* Carl Sandburg's Lincoln.

Two on the Aisle **World Premieres**

W hen NBC introduced *Saturday Night at the Movies* in 1961, it was a daring innovation. The films went on at 9:00 P.M., and for the first time, feature motion pictures became an established element of prime-time air fare. Subsequently, the other networks followed suit, and today movies for TV have become a staple of all network programming.

When it all began on NBC, there was a vast supply of old and not so old feature films to draw on. Yet the supply was not inexhaustible. Perceiving the day when the bottom of the barrel would begin to show, the networks began to sound out Hollywood production companies about the prospects of making feature movies specially for TV. The producers were rightfully chary at first. It was not clear that a major motion-picture studio could produce a movie for television on budgets that could be· but a fraction of those normal to feature films. Cranking out episodes of *Maverick*, *Gunsmoke*, or *Bonanza* on the back lot was one thing. That could be profitable—like a B movie "quickie." But the new proposition was something else again. Gradually, discussions grew more serious and detailed, scripts were analyzed, types of shooting and locations were investigated, and it slowly became clear that with careful calculation, TV movies could be made without financial disaster.

In the mid sixties, NBC initiated the production of movies made especially for TV, launching an operation with the working title of *Project 120* (for 120 minutes) in conjunction with Universal Pictures, the production company. Special films for television were subsequently given their current title, *World Premieres*, and eventually a number of major Hollywood studios became involved in their production. After an initial shakedown, both NBC and the studios came to feel quite comfortable with the new arrangement, which gave the network control over theme and subject matter. As with dramatic specials, these productions proved attractive to stars because they were akin to motion pictures and could provide substantial parts.

One of the earliest *Project 120* shows, produced by Universal in 1966, was *Prescription Murder*, adapted from a play by Richard Levinson and William Link. In it a wealthy psychiatrist, who has murdered his wife, is confronted by a bumbling, disheveled, and deferential detective named Columbo. The character of Columbo was fascinating and seemed to be a perfect subject for a TV series. Therefore, NBC-Universal produced a two-hour pilot film, *Ransom for a Dead Man*, starring Peter Falk as Columbo, and that evolved into the worldwide hit *Columbo*.

All sorts of dramatic subjects were ideal for first-rate, entertaining world premieres, and movies for TV proved to be highly attractive vehicles for Hollywood's finest talent. In *Fame is the Name of the Game* (1966), Anthony Franciosa played a reporter for a weekly magazine called *Fame* (which was somewhat reminiscent of *Life*). While on an assignment, he accidentally discovers the body of a murdered girl—which launches a complex plot of mystery and suspense. The film introduced an attractive newcomer, Susan Saint James, who subsequently became the wife (opposite Rock Hudson) in *McMillan and Wife*. *Fame is the Name of the Game* was shortened to *The Name of the Game* for a weekly series in which Franciosa alternated as star with Gene Barry and Robert Stack. Later that year came *The Doomsday Flight*, a drama by Rod Serling about a bomb-carrying New York-to-Los Angeles jetliner. Van Johnson played the captain of the airplane, Edmond O'Brien was the

Top: Peter Falk first appeared as a somewhat bumbling, unsophisticated detective, here with Lee Grant whom he finally arrested, in Ransom for a Dead Man. *Columbo, the character he played, became so popular the show was put into a continuing series and played worldwide. Above: The Silence, the true story of a West Point Cadet silenced for allegedly cheating on an exam, starred Richard Thomas as Cadet James Pelosi. Opposite: Tony Franciosa and Jill St. John run for safety on* Fame is the Name of the Game, *a successful pilot.*

disgruntled bomber demanding $100,000 ransom, and Jack Lord had the role of the FBI agent trying to run down the bomber while there was still time. An altimeter was attached to the bomb to trigger it when the jet landed at Los Angeles near sea level. This was discovered at the last minute, and the flight was diverted to Denver, the "mile high" city (altitude 5,280 feet), thus thwarting the bomber's scheme.

The following year, Doug McClure, Ricardo Montalban, and Katharine Ross teamed up as three people on the run in *The Longest Hundred Miles*, about the efforts of three fugitives to escape Japanese soldiers in the Philippines during World War II. Shortly thereafter came *Ironside*, with Raymond Burr as a detective permanently confined to a wheelchair as the result of a gunshot wound, who sets out to

identify his assailant. In this instance, the movie was a pilot for the later one-hour weekly series. Another acclaimed feature of the same season was *Stranger on the Run*, an offbeat Western set in the bleak railroad town of Banner, New Mexico, in 1885, starring Henry Fonda, Anne Baxter, Michael Parks, Dan Duryea, and Sal Mineo.

A novel world premiere of 1969 was actually a trilogy by Rod Serling: *Night Gallery*. It was made up of three separate stories, each one about people driven by greed and guilt and the resultant ironic relationships. It, too, had a star-studded cast, including Joan Crawford, Richard Kiley, Roddy McDowall, Barry Sullivan, Ossie Davis, and the venerable Sam Jaffe, and it ultimately led to the mystery show *Rod Serling's Night Gallery*. Another movie of that year was *The Whole World is Watching*, written by Richard Levinson

Clockwise from right: Lloyd Bridges and Shirley Jones discover each other in Silent Night, Lonely Night; *Burl Ives played a lawyer in* The Whole World is Watching, *which eventually became* The Bold Ones; *Al Freeman, Jr., and Patty Duke in* My Sweet Charlie; *Martin Sheen in the award-winning* The Execution of Private Slovik.

196

Opposite: Anthony Hopkins as Bruno Hauptmann, in the 3-hour Lindbergh Kidnapping Case. Left: Raymond Massey appearing in a Night Gallery episode, a successful pilot for Rod Serling. Below: Stranger on the Run, set in Mexico in 1855, starred Henry Fonda.

and William Link, about a group of lawyers and their difficulties defending a college student who has been accused of killing a campus policeman. It starred Burl Ives, Joseph Campanella, James Farentino, and Hal Holbrook, and led to the lawyer's segment of *The Bold Ones*.

Though world premieres are well done and extremely popular, they often stick to comparatively safe subjects. This is not always the case. In *Silent Night, Lonely Night*, Lloyd Bridges played a man spending a weekend in a New England town while visiting his wife in a sanitarium—after she has attempted suicide. He loves her deeply but is despondent over this turn of events. By chance he meets a woman (Shirley Jones) who is visiting her son in prep school. She has just learned that her husband has been unfaithful, and she is contemplating divorce. The upshot is a weekend affair, reminiscent of Noel Coward's *Brief Encounter*, between two very lonely, distraught people. It was a poignant film and demonstrated that television could deal dramatically with intimate, sensitive human relationships in a manner acceptable to the diverse, mass audience.

Another milestone production was *My Sweet Charlie*. From almost any point of view, *Charlie* was a tough story for television to handle. It was about a pregnant white teenager who runs away from home and hides in a deserted house on the Gulf Coast. Shortly thereafter, a fugitive black activist, Charlie, breaks into the house and the two confront each other. She is bright, he is articulate, and each is bigoted in a way toward the other.

Universal and NBC agreed to let Levinson and Link take a chance with the unusual script, and the pair headed for the Gulf Coast with actress Patty Duke to play the teenager and Al Freeman, Jr., cast as the black radical. The show was telecast in January, 1970. The critics gave it a rave, the ratings were sensational. *My Sweet Charlie* won three Emmys. *Charlie* was a breakthrough, suggesting that TV films could tackle all sorts of character and social situations as well as the traditional action dramas.

Meanwhile Levinson and Link were interested in yet another property: *The Execution of Private Slovik*, a book by William Bradford Huie. It was the story of the first execution of an American soldier for desertion since the Civil War. Slovik was a born loser and petty criminal who was drafted toward the end of World War II and shipped overseas. He refused to fire a rifle, deserted, was caught, and was sentenced to be executed. In due time, he was dispatched by a firing squad. It was a terrible affair. Slovik could have returned to combat and saved himself, but he refused. During Eisenhower's presidency the story had been taboo because Ike had been the Supreme Commander when Slovik was executed. Then, just before Kennedy was elected, Frank Sinatra picked up the option to do the story as a feature film and announced that he was going to produce *Slovik*. Sinatra ultimately abandoned the option, Universal picked it up, and Levinson and Link produced *The Execution of Private Slovik* for NBC. *Slovik* won a George Foster Peabody Award, the most prestigious honor any television show can receive.

The recent three-hour *Lindbergh Kidnapping Case* unfolded in realistic detail all the horrible trappings of that tragic event of the thirties, including a uniquely American carnival atmosphere. The question of whether Bruno Richard Hauptmann (played by Anthony Hopkins) was actually the kidnapper was resurrected.

Among the 1975-76 season standouts dealing with sensitive and serious social issues were *The Secret Night Caller*, about the rising incidence of obscene telephone calls and the neurotic impulses that prompt them; *Farewell to Manzanar*, an examination of the plight of the many Japanese-Americans who were stuffed into internment camps at the start of World War II; and *Judge Horton and the Scottsboro Boys*, about the case of the nine black youths accused of the rape of two white girls in Tennessee in the 1930s, in which Judge James Horton, who presided over their trials, sacrificed a promising career to the cause of equal justice.

NBC's World Premieres, combined with the showings of first-rate films *not* made for TV *(The Godfather* and *The Sound of Music*, for example), have truly created what Bob Hope refers to as the "motion-picture theater right in our own home."

Sitcom
Weekly Comedy

In 1949, *The Life of Riley,* Jackie Gleason's radio show, moved to television. The old family situation comedy did not fare very well in the new medium, at least with Gleason as its chief character. After a few struggling months, William Bendix took over as Riley, and a bit later, the show took off for a long and successful run. Since then, many weekly comedy shows have struggled. Some have failed, others have been spectacularly successful.

In 1951, CBS discovered the talents of Lucille Ball and Desi Arnaz. *I Love Lucy* reruns can be seen today. NBC came up with a discovery of its own—Wally Cox, who played the eccentric, loveable teacher *Mr. Peepers.* The show was live, a half-hour on Sunday nights, and usually found Mr. Peepers in one predicament or another. Getting things untangled frequently required the help of his friend the gym teacher (Tony Randall), or his girlfriend (Pat Benoit). The situations generally involved such locales as the principal's office, the gym, and the boardinghouse where Mr. Peepers lived, which was presided over by a very funny, stuttering landlady, Mrs. Gurney, played, of course, by Marion Lorne.

Riley was not the only radio show transferred to TV. *Amos 'n' Andy,* this time with an all-black cast, proved quite adaptable to the new medium, though as times changed it began to seem stereotyped and was phased out. The format

that dominated the scene through the fifties and into the sixties was the family situation comedy. One of the first was *The Goldbergs,* also over from radio. It was a gentle Jewish family situation, very much New York and quite thick in ethnic accent, with Gertrude Berg playing Molly the matriarch, as she had for so long on radio. Other staples in the cast were her husband Jake (played by Robert H. Harris), Uncle David (Eli Mintz), and daughter Rosalie (Arlene McQuade), whose activities, friendships, and relationships were frequently the focus of family concern. A hallmark of the show, which occurred for any of numerous reasons, was that moment when Molly went to the window and called out to her neighbor: "Yoohoo! Mrs. Bloom!"

Another radio carry-over in the same vein was *The Aldrich Family,* which generally revolved around the activities of the family's teenage son, Henry (Bobby Ellis), and his buddy Homer. It, too, had a verbal tribal call. Henry's mother (Barbara Robbins) would call from the house: "Heeenn-ri!" Whereupon Henry would respond: "Coming, Mother!" Henry's father, by the way, was played by House Jamison who had also starred in the show on radio.

Most family comedies of the fifties were matriarchal, and the husbands were generally bumbling idiots to one degree or another. But there were exceptions. For some years, Robert Young played a strong, patient, and wise par-

Opposite: Wally Cox gets into another jam as the mild-mannered teacher Mr. Peepers. Left: "Yoohoo! Mrs. Bloom," yells Molly Goldberg from the window of her apartment on the show The Goldbergs, a radio program originally. Below: a trivia feast—Gloria Winters, Jackie Gleason, and Rosemary DeCamp (later to play Bob Cummings's sister) in their roles as Babs, Chester A., and Peg Riley on The Life of Riley's very first telecast in 1949.

ent on *Father Knows Best,* a program that shuttled back and forth between NBC and CBS. Though in each episode pandemonium of one sort or another broke loose, father managed to keep his head while everyone around him was losing his. And generally, his level head prevailed in the end, proving that father did indeed know best. In fact, the advice he gave is just as valid today as it was then, attested to by the number of reruns of the show that can be seen sometime during the day in almost any city in the country. Besides good advice, the show has also provided a feast for trivia lovers, the most common question being: who were the members of the family and who played them? A bit more difficult: in what town did the family live? Very difficult: who played a construction surveyor boyfriend of Betty's on two shows? Answers: The Andersons, Jim, Margaret, Betty, Bud, and Kathy (Kitten, to Jim), were played by Young, Jane Wyatt, Elinor Donahue, Billy Gray, and Laurin Chapin; Springfield; Roger Smith.

A strong NBC lead of the time was Bob Cummings, who played a kind of male Lucille Ball on *The Bob Cummings Show.* His role was that of a photographer, who was surrounded by gorgeous models and had a homely assistant (Ann B. Davis as Schultzie) running his studio in love with him. It was one predicament after another usually involving one or more of the models.

By today's standards, comedy in the fifties was bland, just as weekly drama was (it's a long way from *Barney Blake* to *Police Story*). The situations could hardly be said to have had significant human dimensions. They were, as Norman Lear has put it, mostly at a level of concern such as "Will Mother burn the Sunday roast?" *Amos 'n' Andy* were stereotypes, as were others (*Riley, The Goldbergs*). Their jokes were mostly white jokes—quite a contrast to Fred Sanford's humor, which taps a wealth of genuine ethnic material.

But in the sixties, all that began to change, and new kinds of comedy situations opened up. *Car 54, Where Are You?* was an early switch. Though it was still very much a

Clockwise from opposite top: The radio Aldrich Family*—House Jamison (right) was the only one to make it to TV; Robert Young on set of* Father Knows Best; *Bob Cummings and Ann B. Davis on opposite sides of the blond; the Baxter family— Whitney Blake, Don DeFore, Shirley Booth, and Bobby Buntrock.*

situation show, it was also something else: a takeoff on Jack Webb's deadpan *Dragnet.* It featured Fred Gwynne and Joe E. Ross as two cops in a prowl car, working out of a Bronx precinct. The former was tall, skinny, and homely; the latter was short and stocky—giving the pair an Abbott and Costello resemblance, which carried through because they were a pair of inveterate bunglers. When called in an emergency, Car 54 could be counted on to botch the job. The two cops, Officers Muldoon and Toody, might be preoccupied with fixing a flat, for instance. And when they did get rolling, everything went wrong anyway. On one occasion, they were supposed to assist in evicting a stubborn lady from her apartment. The pair ended up taking her side against the landlord.

Another successful spoof of the sixties was *Get Smart,* a takeoff on the James Bond 007 craze. It took all the Bond characters and turned them inside out. "Control" (the good guys) and "Kaos" (the bad guys) were both in for trouble when Maxwell Smart (Secret Agent 86—Don Adams), and his attractive associate, "99" (Barbara Feldon), set out together (along with Spy Dog, K-13) for a day's work. Smart's number is derived from an old barroom expression: "getting eighty-sixed" in a saloon means being thrown out as hopelessly drunk. In the show, Maxwell Smart was constantly in jeopardy of being eighty-sixed, for a variety of zany reasons, all unrelated to alcohol. He frequently signed off a bungled job with a call to Control: "Sorry about that, Chief."

Another very successful show of the sixties was *Hazel.* The title role, rare for television in those days, was played by a first-class Broadway actress and Academy Award winner, Shirley Booth, who felt a strong affinity for the central character. Hazel was a domineering maid. The prototype for the character was taken from the Ted Key cartoons that were

once an established feature of the old *Saturday Evening Post.* Hazel ran the household and bossed everyone about —mother, father, and a young son. Everything revolved around Hazel. Everything.

I Dream of Jeannie was innovative in a different direction. The show was, quite literally, out of this world. Jeannie was a genie right out of Aladdin's lamp. But instead of being a benevolent, miracle-working giant, like Daddy Warbucks's sidekick Punjab, this genie was a very cute Barbara Eden. In the show, she played the devoted slave of actor Larry Hagman (Mary Martin's son), who in turn played a military officer, attached to the space program, who was forever finding himself in one or another acutely embarrassing situation. The predicaments were usually of Jeannie's making, but because of her magical powers, she always managed to extricate her master at the last moment.

Julia was another unique show of the time, unique because it was the first series to star a black actress. The attractive Diahann Carroll played a nurse on the program who was widowed and had a son. She worked for an irascible, but loving, company doctor (Lloyd Nolan). She and her son lived in a rather nice apartment with white neighbors, and the boy had a white playmate. Julia's relationship with her short-fused employer, her neighbors, and her struggle to survive and rear her child, all made for warm and amusing situations that were basically non-racial in character.

In the late sixties, when the whole nation was learning that the so-called hard hats were real people with real concerns, CBS made a big breakthrough in situation comedy ("sitcom") with *All in the Family.* It was Norman Lear's first big comedy hit, an adaptation of a show that had been a stunning success in England about a blue-collar bigot, titled *Till Death Us Do Part.* The problems dealt with in Archie

206

Bunker's world, mostly involving his prejudices against other ethnic groups, other religions, women, and most normal people, were a big step toward reality from those that concerned the one-dimensional people in the sitcoms of the fifties. Shortly thereafter, Lear created a big comedy hit for NBC, starring Redd Foxx and Demond Wilson. *Sanford and Son* was also a British derivative, this time of the cockney show *Steptoe and Son*. But Lear converted it into a comedy about blacks, making the life and times and the prejudices and foibles of Fred Sanford much closer to racial reality than the old blackface world of *Amos 'n' Andy*. Because *Sanford and Son* was immensely popular, NBC also bought a show starring one of the young talents Bob Hope is so high on, Freddie Prinze. Costarring Jack Albertson, the

show was called *Chico and the Man*. Prinze, a Puerto Rican who first made his mark as an ethnic stand-up comedian in New York, portrayed a Mexican-American who cajoled Albertson into giving him a job in the latter's filling station in Southern California.

Because many of today's comedies have moved closer to reality, the characters in them (aside from being funny) are both more convincing and more interesting. For this reason, when a network has a really big comedy hit, the secondary characters may prove solid and popular enough to lead successful lives of their own—hence, spin-offs. *Grady* was a short-lived spin-off from *Sanford and Son*. In 1976, there were at least seven such spin-offs, all from comedies.

Top: I Dream of Jeannie*'s Barbara Eden plays havoc with Larry Hagman (Mary Martin's son in real life) and Sammy Davis, Jr. Opposite: Redd Foxx and Demond Wilson enjoy themselves on the lot in* Sanford and Son.

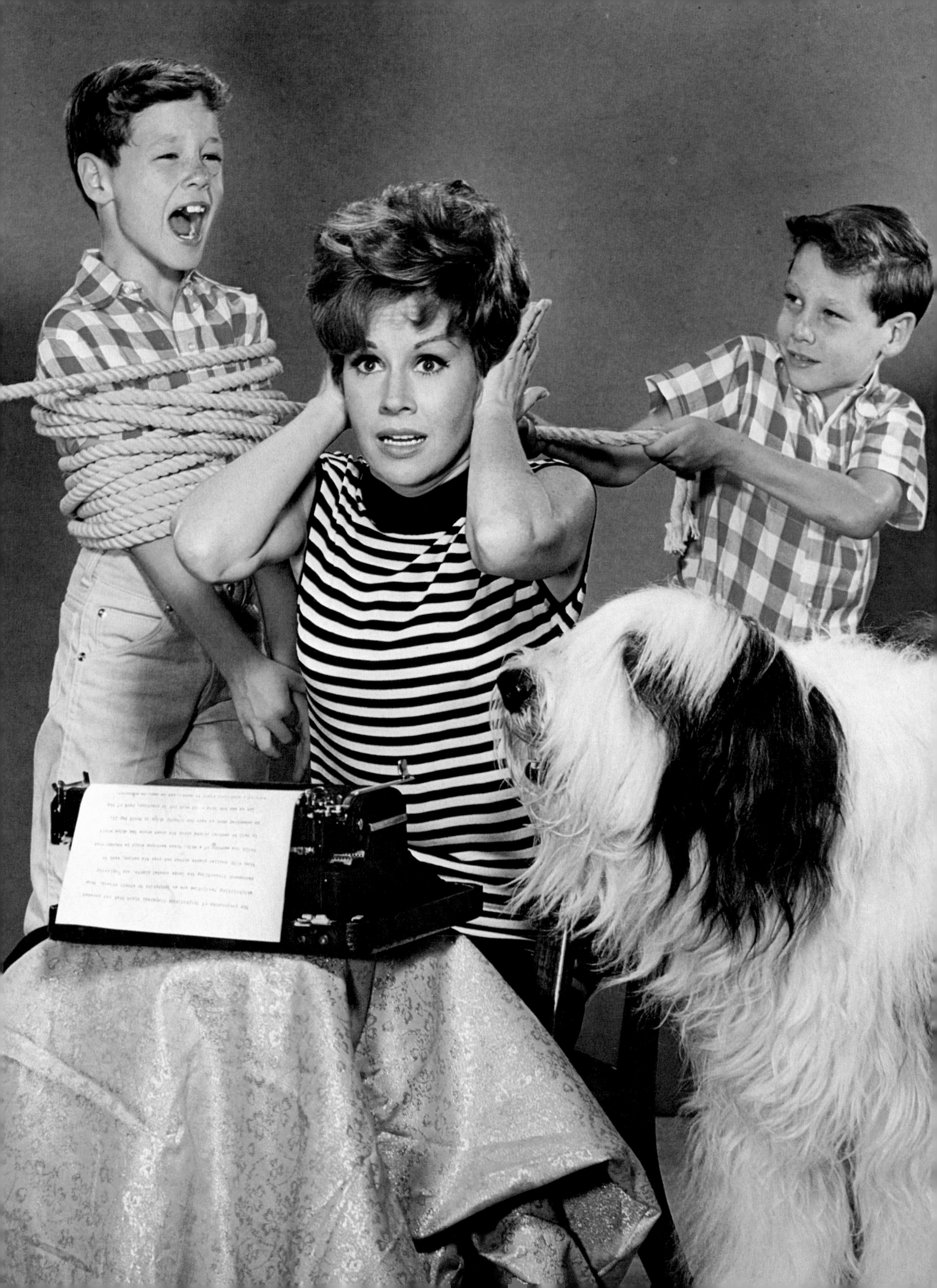

Opposite: Please Don't Eat the Daisies *was television's adaptation of Jean Kerr's Broadway play. It starred Joe and Jeff Fithian as the boys and Patricia Crowley. Above: Don De Fore and Oscar-winning Shirley Booth in NBC's* Hazel.

Clockwise from right: Hope Lange looks for spirits on The Ghost and Mrs. Muir; *Eve Arden and Kay Ballard fight it out in* The Mothers-in-Law; *Danny Thomas and Shelley Fabares talk it over in* The Practice; *Michael Callan and Patricia Harty fake it in* Occasional Wife.

When The Monkees *(below)* went off the air, NBC received the greatest short-term blitz of protesting letters in its history. Get Smart *(opposite)* can be viewed today on reruns and many of Adams's expressions are still around.

Your Show
of Shows
Variety
and
Entertainment

Freddie Prinze and Jack Albertson co-star in Chico and
the Man. Prinze, a comic, was "discovered" for the
show. Albertson, a veteran actor, won the Emmy
in 1976 for his portrayal of an irascible gas-station owner.

n 1948, a show appeared on NBC called *Texaco Star Theater.* On it was a young man with a toothy, Bugs Bunny face named Milton Berle, who would soon be known to kids as "Uncle Miltie" and to an equal multitude of adults simply as "Mr. Television." For many years, Milton Berle was television's top banana. In 1950, when Bob Hope, who was already a name in practically every American household from radio days, made his TV debut Easter Sunday evening, NBC proudly observed that he had scored a whopping Hooper rating of 49.9 percent (in four major cities selected for the survey). That, the network noted, put Hope second only to Milton Berle. As the host of his show, Berle had a variety of notable singers, dancers, and comics as guests, but his real stock-in-trade, at which audiences howled, was slapstick. Uncle Miltie dressed in outlandish outfits. He appeared with Martha Raye (the comedienne whose own stock-in-trade was looking somewhat like a stranded large-mouthed bass) in baggy pants, derby, and cane, in a takeoff of Charlie Chaplin comedies. With the boxer-turned-comic Slapsie Maxie Rosenbloom, he did a parody of the balcony scene from *Romeo and Juliet,* with Slapsie dressed as Romeo and Miltie on the balcony gowned as a coy Juliet. On still another occasion, he came on dressed as Ali Baba.

Not that Milton Berle monopolized the new medium. There were many other first-rate variety shows on the air in the early days. One particularly memorable show, produced by Max Liebman, bowed in 1949 as *Sid Caesar's Admiral Broadway Review.* The following year, it became *Your Show of Shows,* with Caesar and that very funny lady, Imogene Coca. It was a ninety-minute, prime-time affair, presented in a legitimate theater. Guests received printed programs just as they would for a Broadway show. *Your Show* had a different star host or hostess each week, its own group of singers, and a twelve-member dance troupe.

Aside from all sorts of comic skits, pantomimes, routines, and musical numbers done by the two stars, their guests, and the ensemble, there were interludes of classical and semiclassical arias and songs. And among the show's half-dozen writers was Mel Brooks.

A big show originating that same year was the *Colgate Comedy Hour,* produced by that notable showman Mike Todd, who over the years masterminded many a spectacular: a serious *G.I. Hamlet* with Maurice Evans, for the troops in World War II, that cinematic "happening" called *Cinerama,* the feature film *Around the World in 80 Days,* and a marriage to Elizabeth Taylor. The *Comedy Hour* featured rotating comedians each week, among them Eddie Cantor, Fred Allen, Bob Hope, and Abbott and Costello. The program became a showcase for many lesser-known comics who later became famous, notably a couple of youngsters fresh off the borscht circuit in the Catskills, Dean Martin and Jerry Lewis. Others who starred on the show were Donald O'Connor and Danny Thomas. Fred Allen's radio show featured *Allen's Alley* (with a constellation of hilarious characters like Senator Beauregard Claghorn, Titus Moody, Mr. Ajax Cassidy, and Mrs. Pansy Nussbaum) and had drawn a loyal following over the years. It fared badly on TV.

Originally the *Comedy Hour* was telecast from New York. But by 1952, AT&T had installed coast-to-coast coaxial cables and the show moved to Hollywood. Transcontinental radio programming had been routine for years because ordinary telephone lines could carry the shows. Television signals were considerably more complex and required a much wider band of frequencies, which only the new coaxial cable could provide. NBC's studio, station KNBH, was located at a well-known Hollywood intersection, Sunset and Vine. To produce the *Comedy Hour,* a new network operation was set up in a nearby theater, the *El Capitan,* which was located on an even more famous corner:

TV variety in the late 1940s
and early 1950s was
usually zany and slapstick.
Clockwise from above:
Fred Allen carried on a running
feud with Jack Benny;
Sid Caesar and Imogene Coca
kept a frenetic pace on
Your Show of Shows; Milton
Berle got laughs in
costume and in pie face, but
Uncle Miltie soon became
known as "Mr. Television," with
the Texaco Star Theater.

Hollywood and Vine. The show went on the air live at 5:00 P.M. each Sunday, which put it solidly in prime time in the East: eight o'clock.

In the fall of 1951, NBC, realizing that one Hollywood theater would never provide the West Coast studio space the network would soon need, acquired a large tract of land at Burbank, a few miles outside Hollywood, and began building two more. One studio was primarily built for Bob Hope. At first, he wanted an orchestra pit in front of the stage, because that had been a characteristic of all the great vaudeville theaters. But then Hope decided a pit was inappropriate to the new medium; it was omitted. Seats for the audience were placed close to the front of the stage, with a ramp in the middle for a camera. Another studio was fashioned for Red Skelton. Skelton felt a different arrangement would work, so the audience sat in a balcony opposite the stage, and the cameras were placed underneath the balcony. Two other studios were added later.

In 1951, Berle did the very first telethon, for the Damon Runyon Cancer Fund, commemorating the writer whose oddball Broadway characters became the basis for *Guys and Dolls*. A year later, Ralph Edwards was on NBC-TV with a show that he had created earlier for radio and that became so popular it ran for a decade: *This Is Your Life*. The show recreated the life of its guests, surprising them by producing in the studio a parade of old friends and childhood sweethearts, relatives, teachers, and others out of the past. No guest knew who would turn up, which made for some emotional reunions.

The early 1950s featured a variety of musical offerings: *The Voice of Firestone* on NBC presented classical and semiclassical music. The network also had *The Kate Smith Hour*, Perry Como's *Kraft Music Hall*, and *The Dinah Shore Show*, all of which presented musical variety. A big favorite, as it had been on NBC radio, was *Your Hit Parade*, which charted the rise and fall of the top ten song hits every week. Moving the show to television presented problems. The producers felt that each song should be visualized in some way—and differently each week. But when a hit hung up there in the top ten week after week, as some did, brains were wracked to come up with a new visual. When *Mona Lisa* hit the top it was simple enough to show the painting, but when the song persisted on the charts, it presented problems. One week the picture came to life; another week a small boy walked by it in a museum; a third week it was dramatized. When the tune *Harbor Lights* (from the feature film *The Long Voyage Home*) maintained a top rating week after week, enough nautical scenes were used to have made a mini-feature.

The late fifties brought still more musical events. NBC's Mitch Miller offered *Sing Along with Mitch*, which did choral arrangements of popular tunes, both new and old. The program is currently generating nostalgia albums. *The Bell Telephone Hour*, long a network radio staple, presented

Clockwise from left: As Liberace became the idol of millions, his piano, dress, and finger adornments became increasingly more luxurious; Danny Thomas was one of the early guests on the extremely popular Colgate Comedy Hour; *Red Skelton made frequent appearances on the network as did the up-and-coming comedy team of Dean Martin and Jerry Lewis; Ted Mack's* Amateur Hour *featured a classic in unsophisticated advertising.*

221

much classical and semiclassical music. One of the program's frequent guests was a well-liked operatic soprano, Florence Henderson, who years later was to become the mother of ABC's *The Brady Bunch*.

In the mid-fifties, NBC introduced a show with TV's first black host, the very popular singer Nat "King" Cole. It was a half-hour show, in prime time, 7:30 P.M. on Tuesdays. The network could not find sponsors for such a program in those days, but it went on the air anyway. At the regional level, the show did pick up local advertising. Some years later, in the 1965-66 season, NBC again built a musical-variety show around a black host, the irrepressible and very talented Sammy Davis, Jr. And that genius of comedy, Flip Wilson, established once and for all (if it ever needed proving in the first place) that a black host could carry a weekly show right

into the top ratings and hold it there month after month. *The Flip Wilson Show* used theater-in-the-round staging. Flip usually opened the show with an easy narrative monologue and then moved into a series of sketches with his guests, taking on such zany roles of his own invention as "Geraldine" and "Reverend Leroy."

In the sixties, *That Was The Week That Was* (*TW3* for short), adapted for the network from the British show of the same name, took satiric shots at almost everything. The show was short-lived, but it bequeathed an important residual: it made David Frost a star in America. It was also the forerunner of *Rowan & Martin's Laugh-In*, a spectacularly successful variety show. *Laugh-In*, to a large degree the creation of its producer, George Schlatter, was a landmark in the evolution of television programming. It was a unique

type of comedy program, the first of its kind, a show propelled by its material and its format rather than by comedy stars—though it certainly had them in the troupe. *Laugh-In* was a zany montage of one-line quips and questions, film clips, quick cuts and crossover jokes, comic vignettes and pop-up characters. One of its stars, Goldie Hawn, went on to feature films, including *Shampoo*. Henry Gibson, who did weird poems on the show, became the star of *Nashville*. Ruth Buzzi played a little old lady continually in conflict with Arte Johnson, who turned up in various manifestations on the show. One of his most famous was as a World War II German soldier, peering from behind a palm tree muttering, in a heavy accent, "verrry interesting." Another was his "dirty old man" sitting on a park bench, for instance, flirting ponderously with Ruth, only to forget himself, doze off, and

topple off the bench or have her belt him with her purse. *Laugh-In* was fast, unpredictable, side-splitting, and one of NBC's most spectacular successes.

Throughout the sixties and into the seventies, NBC came up with many other highly popular variety shows. One of the hit recording groups of the late fifties and early sixties was the Williams Brothers Quartet. In 1963, Andy was given his own show on NBC. He regularly featured what was then a group of children: the Osmond Brothers. At Christmas time, the whole Williams family gathered on Andy's show to present hits the brothers had recorded in years past.

Two other popular musical shows of the period were hosted on NBC by Perry Como and Dean Martin. On *The Dean Martin Show*, Dean opened with a good monologue and did sketches with his guests, who were often other

Clockwise from left: Perry Como rolled up his sleeves and belted out weekly song favorites; Ernie Kovacs displayed his particular brand of craziness on The Ernie Kovacs Show; *Kate Smith opened with "When the Moon Comes Over the Mountain"; Eddie Fisher's talent and well-publicized love affairs brought him to the top of television popularity.*

comedians: Bob Hope, Flip Wilson, *Laugh-In*'s Rowan and Martin—and always, pretty girls. Unlike Flip and others, Martin played himself. It was a characteristic Martin affair, and it was very popular into the early seventies. At that point, Dean then turned to occasional specials and his celebrated "Roasts."

In recent years, aside from specials featuring Dean Martin, Elvis Presley, Ann-Margret, Andy Williams, and others, weekly variety shows have become less prominent in the NBC schedule, though the network continues to look for new hits.

In the heyday of radio, NBC's New York studios were alive with music, from combos and society orchestras in the small studios, to the big NBC Symphony under Arturo Toscanini in Studio 8-H. Fully a third of the network's radio

Martha Raye (top) made the most of her offbeat looks and outgoing personality. Her guest list included the Gabor sisters. Mitch Miller (above) took time off from his Sing Along With Mitch *show in 1961 to telecast a Christmas special. Elvis Presley (opposite) appeared often on television, but when he first sang over a network broadcast, only the top half of his body was seen.*

programming was music. When television was born, it was only natural that this great musical reservoir should be tapped for special entertainment. In 1948, Toscanini conducted Beethoven's Ninth Symphony, letting the small number of TV viewers of the day hear and see it for the first time outside a concert hall. That same year, two of Gian Carlo Menotti's popular and short contemporary operas, *The Telephone,* and later in the year *The Medium,* were piped live from Philadelphia. The following year, Leonard Bernstein led the Boston Symphony in a special tribute to the then-fledgling United Nations. NBC established its own television opera company, too, for which Menotti wrote a special Christmas opera for children, *Amahl and the Night Visitors.* Over the years, the NBC Opera presented a great deal of the classic operatic repertory in English—*La Bohème, The Magic Flute, Boris Godunov, Fidelio,* and *Don Giovanni,* to name but a few. But as the sixties approached, and the total television audience was expanding enormously, the audience for the NBC Opera did not increase. The number of original productions diminished, and because of the flagging audience interest the company was ultimately disbanded.

In 1955, a new NBC television format called *Producer's Showcase,* which had gone on the air the previous year to offer well-known dramas each month, presented the celebrated British dance company, the Sadler's Wells Ballet, in Tchaikovsky's *Sleeping Beauty.* Two years later, *Showcase* offered another noted British production, the Royal Ballet's *Cinderella.* Also in 1957, Hallmark made the first of a number of moves from drama into the musical field by sponsoring one of the finest of all the Gilbert and Sullivan operettas, *The Yeomen of the Guard.* In 1964, Hallmark produced yet another notable musical, *The Fantasticks.*

In 1953, the Ford Motor Company celebrated its fiftieth anniversary with NBC, and the result was quite a show. The cast included Mary Martin, Ethel Merman, Ed Murrow (CBS's celebrated *See It Now* reporter, on loan for the occasion), Oscar Hammerstein II, Kukla, Fran and Ollie, and Wally Cox. The following year, the network itself introduced a new type of entertainment program, to which it gave the title *The Sunday Spectacular.* These were actually big, splashy productions in the Broadway theatrical sense. They were ninety minutes long (7:30-9:00 P.M.), in color. The first of the color spectaculars, under the aegis *Max Liebman Presents,* was an original musical comedy called *Satins and Spurs,* starring Betty Hutton. Appropriately, it was produced in NBC's biggest New York studio, a vast building in Brooklyn that had formerly been the old Vitagraph Studios in the early feature-film days. (It now houses *Another World,* with its many sets, and is sometimes used for special productions.) In *Satins and Spurs,* Hutton played a rodeo star, Cindy Smathers, who came to New York to compete at Madison Square Garden. *Life* photographers were influential in those days, so appropriately enough, the plot revolved around the efforts of one of them (Tony Bart, played by Kevin McCarthy) to shoot a photo layout on the star. After the show, Steve Allen appeared on the big Brooklyn stage to give the viewing audience a brief tour, pointing out that this was the largest TV studio in the world. Then the program closed with a reminder to watch the next spectacular on NBC, which would be *Lady in the Dark,* with Ann Sothern.

NBC also had its *Producer's Showcase,* in color and in two hours of prime time, with the full Broadway production of *Peter Pan,* starring Mary Martin. The program was a spec-

Clockwise from left: Uncle Miltie celebrates New Year's; Flip Wilson's Geraldine gets it on with Sammy Davis, Jr.; A 1962 Milton Berle Show *satirized filmed historical epics. With Berle, who portrayed Cleopatra, were Jack Benny and Charleton Heston as Ben Hur, and Kirk Douglas and Laurence Harvey as Spartacus; Ernie Ford, Phil Silvers, and Danny Thomas in a* Guys and Dolls *sequence.*

227

Preceding pages: Dan Rowan and Dick Martin on Laugh-In; *Dionne Warwick on* The Flip Wilson Show. *Clockwise from right: Nipsy Russell sticks it to Michael Landon on a Dean Martin Roast; Jack Lemmon brings his musical talents to television; Snoopy at the Ice Follies; Mitch Miller leads his friends on the* Sing Along With Mitch *show.*

tacular success, attracting a then-record audience of 65 million viewers, a shoo-in for an Emmy. It was repeated the following year.

1958 was a vintage year for NBC, notable for a very special evening with a very special gentleman: *An Evening with Fred Astaire*. It was Fred's first live TV show and it was so good it won seven Emmy awards. Another great solo evening came in 1965 when the network presented *Frank Sinatra—A Man and His Music*, a program that was both widely watched and widely acclaimed.

Over the years, a number of specials have become institutionalized at NBC to the point of being annual affairs. The Tournament of Roses Parade from Pasadena, California, preceding the Rose Bowl game on New Year's Day dates back a long way. The Thanksgiving Day Parade is another standard, with its huge floating figures of Mickey Mouse, Underdog, Snoopy, and other cartoon characters. Still another pageant is the *Miss America* affair. It has come a long way from the old days, when it was a rather simple (though nationally promoted) event held on the boardwalk at Atlantic City, New Jersey. Then there is *Ringling Brothers Circus,* which is usually filmed in Sarasota, Florida, before the show goes on the road. Until very recently, *Bob Hope's Christmas Show* was an annual event as well.

What can make a good entertainment special is very much a question of what is good show business at that particular time. It can be quite contemporary, like the show the young and gifted Canadian illusionist Doug Henning did, in 1975, from a sound stage in Culver City, California. It was done before a live audience, because any magic show has to be done that way to have full impact. (If it were done without an audience, it would be all too easy to believe it was rigged.) Henning's show began with some first-rate feats of illusion, including one in which the head, the arms, and the torso of an attractive young lady appeared to become completely severed from each other. But the *pièce de résistance* was his re-creation of the greatest and most baffling of all the feats of the great magician Harry Houdini. Houdini had himself locked in a trunk, and the trunk was then tied up with heavy chains joined with padlocks. Escape was seemingly impossible. To heighten the drama considerably, the whole affair, presumably with Houdini securely locked inside it, was lowered into water, where the magician was sure to either suffocate or drown. Somehow, at the last possible moment, Houdini managed to escape from this impossible situation. Houdini died in 1926, taking his secret with him. No magician tried to repeat the stunt—until Doug Henning.

With members of the Los Angeles Police Department supervising, Henning's feet were placed in heavy stocks and the stocks were secured by chains, a padlock, and screws that could be removed only from the outside. Handcuffs kept his wrists about a foot apart. The stocks, with Henning dangling head downward, were then hoisted up and lowered into a transparent tank of water. The stocks became the top of the tank and were padlocked down. A curtain was drawn around the tank, and a suffocation countdown was begun. As the seconds passed, the audience grew visibly tense and riveted their attention on the tank. Just as time was about to run out, Doug Henning appeared on stage out of nowhere, leaving the audience to gasp with amazement and relief at the sight of the empty tank.

Good entertainment can also be nostalgic, as in *Life Goes to the Movies,* a show built around the symbiotic rela-

tionship between a number of notable *Life* photographers (and a small number of reporters and editors, particularly the late irrepressible Mary Leatherbee, sister of Josh Logan), and the Hollywood world of stars and filmmakers, hoopla and ballyhoo. This was a scene that the magazine explored intimately for years. For many an aspiring starlet or fledgling actor, making the cover of *Life* could do more toward advancing a career than winning an Oscar. With rare still photos and never-before-seen segments of film, *Life Goes to the Movies* created a wonderful montage of that bygone era.

Entertainment can also be timeless, like James Barrie's 1904 play, *Peter Pan*. When Mary Martin did it on the stage, and then for NBC in the fifties, it was very much a song-and-dance adaptation built around Mary as the central star. NBC's new production will be closer to the original play. Some scenes were shot in Kensington Gardens, in London, where Barrie lived and set the original story. The waiflike Mia Farrow, as Peter Pan, seems closer to being a peer of Wendy's than did Mary Martin. Danny Kaye is surely at his most enjoyable as Captain Hook.

Television was originally designed as a medium of entertainment. Both the medium and the entertainment have come a long way. Variety shows and entertainment specials have become a valuable showcase for American, and worldwide, talent.

Opposite: Liza Minnelli was practically a one-person show when she did Liza With a Z, *which featured a number from* Cabaret. *Above: Goldie Hawn went from* Laugh-In *to starring roles in Hollywood movies.*

Below: James Barrie's 1904 play Peter Pan *was reconstructed for the talents of Mary Martin when it was brought to Broadway and to NBC. Opposite top:* Amahl and the Night Visitors *in its seventh year. Opposite bottom: Esther Williams takes the plunge in an entertainment special.*

Opposite: Frank Sinatra and Ella Fitzgerald pool their talents. Top left: Donald O'Connor congratulates Oscar winners William Holden and Donna Reed for their 1953 performances in Stalag 17 *and* From Here to Eternity. *Top right: Humphrey Bogart and Lauren Bacall (Mrs. Bogart) let the television audience into their lives not long before Mr. Bogart succumbed to cancer. Above: Milton Berle conducts marathon for Damon Runyon Fund.*

"Heeeeeere's Johnny!" Late-Night Television

In 1950, when television was in its infancy, the networks went on the air and off again at rather civilized hours, with programming generally starting in late afternoon and ending before midnight. Programming was, by today's standards, almost entirely in prime time. Then NBC began a series of innovative moves to probe the possibilities of the earlier and later parts of the day, which are now referred to as "fringe time." It did not seem like a very propitious move; some thought "preposterous" was the right word. As everyone knows, the viewing habits of many millions of Americans were ultimately changed. Early risers, night owls, and that select few who survive with hardly any sleep at all can now turn on their televisions for entertainment or information according to whim.

June of 1950 saw the launching of *Broadway Open House*, a zany nightclub variety show that was hosted Tuesdays, Thursdays, and Fridays by Jerry Lester, a stand-up comic from Las Vegas. On Mondays and Wednesdays an-

other comedian, Morey Amsterdam, was the emcee. The show had a music group including accordionist Milton De-Lugg and, like many of the night shows that would follow it, featured a number of regulars, the most memorable being a statuesque, well-endowed blond known as Dagmar (Jenny Lewis). Jerry Lester was diminutive, brash, loud. And because he just about came up to Dagmar's "assets," the show was provided with a sight gag. *Open House* was an hour-long program. Because of low budgets, it needed but one sponsor, the Anchor-Hocking Glass Company.

Two years later, the *Today* show with Dave Garroway opened up the early morning hours, and two years after that, on September 27, 1954, *Broadway Open House*, having undergone several metamorphoses, became the *Tonight* show, starring Steve Allen. Viewing time was extended to ninety minutes (11:30 P.M. to 1:00 A.M.), and at first the program originated from a legitimate Broadway theater, the Hudson, near Times Square. (Already television was begin-

Broadway Open House *featured a number of regular performers,*
among them Wayne Howell (opposite, left front row),
host Jerry Lester (in chair), *accordionist Milton DeLugg*
and the well-endowed Dagmar, whose real name was Jenny
Lewis. Above: Fun, games, and zany stunts on Open House.

Steve Allen (above with George Montgomery and Dinah Shore) began the Tonight show in 1954. Later he turned the job over to Jack Paar. Paar's energies were formidable— if the guests couldn't come to him, he came to them. Among those who appeared on television with Paar were (clockwise from opposite top left): Liza Minnelli, Cliff Arquette, Albert Schweitzer, Shelley Winters and Senator John Fitzgerald Kennedy; and Eleanor Roosevelt.

ning to bite into the theater, and a number were closing their doors.) The *Tonight* show with Steve Allen featured Skitch Henderson's orchestra, and it slowly built up a stock company, including Steve Lawrence and Eydie Gorme. The format accommodated all sorts of plugs—for books, movies, shows—with Allen seated comfortably behind a desk. A number of actors, including Tom Poston who is now a perennial guest celebrity, did mock man-on-the-street interviews. At the back of the studio were two huge metal doors, called "elephant doors," which could open out onto the side street and had formerly been used to accommodate sets and scenery brought into the Hudson for legitimate shows. Steve Allen had one camera trained on the elephant doors, and every now and then they would be opened for interviews with passersby on the street. The word got around, and before long the place was overrun with people hanging around in hopes the doors would open.

The show also had its serious side. Steve Allen was a person of considerable social sensitivity and concern and spoke out on a variety of causes, some of which were quite unpopular at the time.

Doing *Tonight* five nights a week proved to be one of the most exhausting acting jobs in television. Because it was live and spontaneous, almost anything could happen— and usually did. After three seasons, Jack Paar took over and gave the show his own special character. He ran a very personal show that reflected his own somewhat testy, touchy, inquisitive personality. One upshot of this was that he frequently ended up in feuds that made the headlines. One memorable ruckus occurred when Paar took the show to West Berlin for a week. The *New York Times*, columnists Walter Winchell, Dorothy Kilgallen, and Irving Kupcinet, and several senators alleged that Paar had used Army facilities for transportation and other favors abroad. (The print media could be vindictive to the threat of the electronic medium in those days.) Returning to the United States, an infuriated and largely innocent Paar took them all on during one show.

Like Steve Allen, Paar built up a company of regulars. And they were a diverse lot. Paar's Ed McMahon was Hugh Downs. Another regular was José Melis, the Cuban piano player, who appeared with his band. There was also the French actress Geneviève, whose accent Paar mimicked. There was broad-humored, American actress Peggy Cass and Dodi Goodman, a compulsive talker. But Paar's *pièce de résistance* was Alexander King, sometime author of offbeat books *(May this House be Safe from Tigers),* former dope addict, and raconteur who professed (not very believably) to have all kinds of inside information on all sorts of famous people.

Paar managed to keep the show going for nearly five years. But finally he, too, had had it. On October 1, 1962, came Johnny. Johnny Carson made the *Tonight* show pure entertainment, with songs, jokes, and skits. He is talented, witty, genial, bright, and almost completely unflappable. And he proved to be a complete genius at handling this type of show. Recognizing how grueling the show is, NBC provided Carson with ample vacations to rest and relax. And along the way, the *Tonight* show became known officially by the much more elaborate and complimentary title: *The Tonight Show Starring Johnny Carson*—even when a substitute host was in the chair. As a consequence, Johnny Carson has become a television institution.

If *The Tonight Show*, on the air, seems casual, relaxed

and spontaneous, this is because it has been meticulously prepared in advance to swing along informally, without lapses, so that it is always "up" and the audience is correspondingly enthusiastic. Aside from the inimitable Carson himself, there are many other critical elements to this particular brew. The show has a staff of fifty to sixty people. The chief of staff is its producer, Fred deCordova. Director Bobby Quinn seems to have an unerring eye for placing cameras. Critical to the operation are five talent coordinators. Individually they conduct in-depth interviews with candidates for the show, determining what they might do or say, show or tell, that will interest, entertain, or amuse. They then prepare a list of questions that Carson may choose from in quizzing his guests. If the guest happens to have written a book it is virtually certain that Johnny will have read it, cover to cover. So these and other factors, including Carson's unique gift for carrying such a show (he has an uncanny ability for putting almost any guest immediately at ease), help *Tonight* to swing along unselfconsciously.

On an average day, show time begins in the early afternoon. A large, private road into NBC's Burbank compound passes between the commissary and the stage entrance to Studio One. Beside the entrance are half a dozen or so

244

When Paar left Tonight, *Johnny Carson* took over. On the very first show, Carson came from behind the curtain to the call of "Heeeeeere's Johnny!" (opposite bottom). The announcer and foil was Ed McMahon (opposite top). Carson's first guest star was Groucho Marx (above). Another guest of frequent appearances is John Wayne.

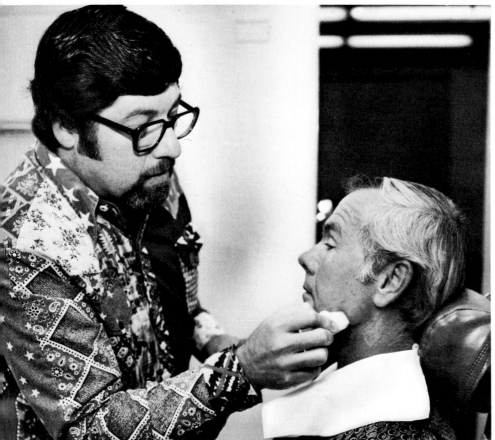

Carson's day begins long before
the actual telecast. It
includes time in the office,
reading the books of
guests, studying the papers,
a conference with his
writers, and, of course, before
the show, a make-up session.

247

parking spaces, each reserved by a white plaque with a gold star and a name on it. The plaque nearest the entrance reads JOHNNY CARSON. The presence of a sleek, green Mercedes coupe reveals that Johnny is in the studio. (On days when someone else is hosting the show the first space will be differently labeled and occupied: McLean Stevenson and his steel-gray Porsche, for instance.) During the first few hours Johnny goes over the monologue with his writers. (His stand-up opening string of jokes and quips, something he and Bob Hope are masters of, is the only part of the show that is written; and the gist of the monologue is inscribed on a long cue board that Carson can refer to from the stage if he wishes, but which the audience cannot see.) He may attend to other matters as well: while in the studio he frequently does public service spots for a variety of causes and charities. Then he goes off to his small but comfortable office, closes the door, and sits alone studying his monologue.

Meanwhile the audience is sitting patiently in the studio while various technicians move about setting lights and mikes and attending to other production details. For visitors at the very back of the audience a number of large TV monitors suspended from the ceiling will provide a better view of the show. In the wings a large coffee urn from the commissary is available for the production crew. On stage, Doc Severinsen and the orchestra rehearse. Then, as show-time approaches, Ed McMahon comes out. He and Doc engage in some banter, the band plays a number or two, and then Ed jokes, quips, and asks questions of the audience. This is known as the "warm-up." The studio audience has been waiting for some time now. Many people may have stood on line outside for up to three hours. Ed and Doc now entertain the audience, get everyone together, and generate a feeling of anticipation for what is to come. Ed McMahon, who (like Carson) has a knack for sensing an audience and whether it is largely youthful, or tourist, or of a mixed assortment, is a master of the warm-up. He may raise anticipation still further by slyly suggesting that possibly Johnny may not really appear, which adds a touch of apprehension that only increases the excitement. Finally, it's show time. The orchestra hits the theme, Ed announces the title and the evening's guests, and then he turns and gestures toward the colorful curtains: "And now, heeere's Johnny!" There is an agonizing and hushed hesitation, and then the man himself appears, to a ringing (and relieved) applause.

The "mileage" that Johnny Carson has chalked up in his fourteen-year tenure on *Tonight* is nothing short of staggering, especially considering the show is taped live and that except for the opening monologue he is on the air, unscripted and unrehearsed, for ninety minutes, day after day, which is both physically and mentally exhausting. He has done about 3,000 shows so far, and it is estimated he has played to about 16 billion viewers, roughly four times the total population of our planet. In setting these track records he has logged more TV time by far than anyone in the history of the medium, including the durable Ed Sullivan (who, because he had a variety show, was not continually on camera). How does he do it? What makes Johnny run?

For one thing he keeps in superb physical condition.

He plays a lot of very fast tennis during his days off. And he does have days off, and liberal vacations as well. Both are quite essential to keeping in top physical and mental form. He also has an amazing talent for his kind of show. Though this is partly a gift, there is much more to it than that. He has studied his craft meticulously. He has also had considerable experience. Johnny Carson was a teenage magician, then a radio announcer, then a local TV personality in Omaha, subsequently putting together different shows of his own. In 1953 he substituted for Red Skelton one night, opening with a monologue he put together while driving to the studio. Commented Jack Benny the next day: "The kid is great, just great." Shortly thereafter CBS hired the kid, and he went on to do a variety of shows on all three networks. Since the mid fifties he has also been playing one-week engagements in Las Vegas to standing-room audiences, a kind of training that, as Bob Hope notes in his foreword, is not unlike that provided by the great old-time incubator known as vaudeville. So when the time came to take over the *Tonight* show, Johnny Carson was ready.

Weekend, an NBC News production which is shown the first Saturday of every month from 11:30 P.M. to 1:00 A.M., like its antecedents, features a great variety of items of varying lengths, gleaned from all over the world. Some are spectacular (such as the killer bees of Brazil), others less so (a feature on the world long-distance frisbee champion). It has profiled Hugh Hefner, the foetal alcohol syndrome, the White House barber, and the unionized Dutch army. There are funny bits of animation. Every now and again, a card with an amusing saying (known as a "verbal") pops on as in an old silent movie. All in all, it is a lively show and deliberately so. In its late-night slot it has to be entertaining, but one can detect in *Weekend* a high level of journalistic perception in the tradition of its producer, Reuven Frank.

Tom Snyder's *Tomorrow,* an interview format aired Monday through Friday at 1:00 A.M., is also a versatile information vehicle. Snyder has taken on Coretta King and critic Walter Kerr, a street gang, even Gloria Swanson. He discusses UFOs, sports gambling, and high-fashion modeling. One entire program originated from a 747 in flight; a series came from Vietnam; *Tomorrow* visited a leper colony; also a nudist colony (filmed from the shoulders up). It is Tom Snyder himself who carries the show. He is an unusual combination of newsman and entertainer. NBC likes him well enough to have given him the anchor position for the second hour of its two-hour evening news program on WNBC-TV, New York.

The Midnight Special, which swings along into the wee hours on Friday nights, is pure entertainment, featuring rock groups, singers, and comics.

The most recent addition to fringe time, *Saturday Night,* is a refreshing novelty—youthful, zany, iconoclastic. As a live show, *NBC's Saturday Night* is a throwback to the earliest days of television and to variety programs like Sid Caesar's and Imogene Coca's *Your Show of Shows.* The program's repertory company, the "Not Ready for Prime Time Players," headed by Chevy Chase, is just as youthful as the writers, and its audacity has attracted a large and loyal audience among young urban adults.

The Midnight Special *swings into the wee hours on Friday nights, is pure entertainment, featuring rock groups, singers, and comics, and hosts such as Chubby Checker.*

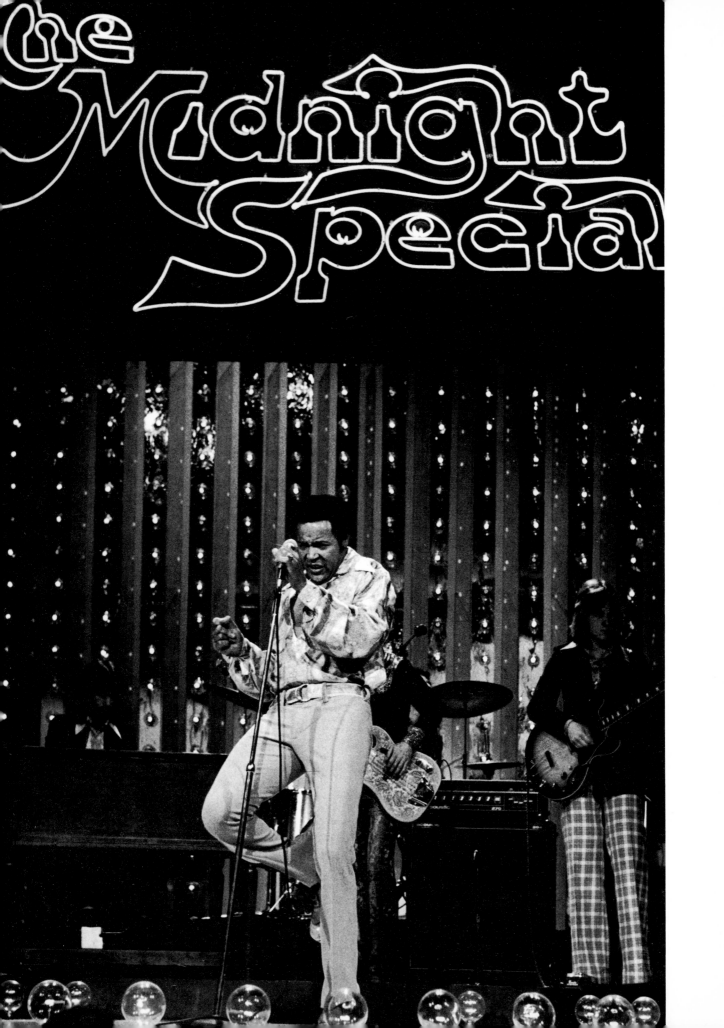

"Letters...
We Get
Letters"
Afterword

Saturday Night *is a novelty—youthful, zany, iconoclastic, and televised live. It features Chevy Chase as an irreverent news reporter who usually trips on his way to the news desk or when receiving an Emmy award.*

Television may now have become the most important institution in American life. A 1975 Harris Survey of the public's confidence in a dozen key institutions, a subject on which the organization has polled people periodically since 1966, shows doctors, educators, and the people who handle television news at the top of the most trusted list. Faith in religion, the United States Supreme Court, and the press has declined somewhat. Confidence in the military, major corporations, and law firms has dropped severely. And less than 15 percent of those polled have much confidence at all in organized labor, the Congress, or the executive branch of the federal government. Contrary to the opinion of many people who felt the mass media were out to "get" President Nixon during the Watergate proceedings, the public's trust in both TV news *and* the press reached a new high during the dramatic year of 1973. Today, television news is the major source of information for the general public. Stations all over the country are expanding their own news staffs to cover the local scene more thoroughly and, along with the network news, are giving the news more air time than ever before—with great success and considerable public approval and acclaim.

News aside, television today is far and away the primary source of entertainment, including participatory sports. The average American now logs twenty-five hours a week watching TV. That amounts to more than three hours a day. More than 200 million Americans do this, courtesy of the more than 960 commercial and noncommercial stations and 121 million television sets abroad in the land. In the whole of human history no other medium of communication comes anywhere near these figures. All the books published in the Western world in a year reach only a fraction of the people touched by broadcasting in a single day! In no other country except Japan is this symbiotic relationship between viewer and set so intense. Some people question whether the relationship is symbiotic at all, in the sense of any real give-and-take between broadcaster and viewer. The late and esteemed columnist Walter Lippmann commented: "While television is supposed to be free, it has in fact become the creature, the servant and indeed the prostitute of merchandising." And the director of the Research Institute of America, Leo Cherne, has observed that broadcasting determines "the way we perceive and the way we think, and most importantly, what we think well of." Adds the poet Archibald MacLeish: "Broadcasting matters more over the long run . . . than what anybody else does because [it is] more persistently shaping the minds of more people than all the rest of us put together." Yet attorney Newton Minow, when he was chairman of the Federal Communications Commission, labeled TV "a vast wasteland."

It is possible to interpret these pronouncements with such a degree of cynicism as to suggest that the medium is completely brainwashing the American people. If that were so we would all now be doomed, already embalmed in George Orwell's mindless world of 1984. Such a view leads to two conclusions, both of which are contrary to fact. One is that television managers and producers are themselves totally cynical. The other and more important conclusion would have to be that the American people are scarcely more independent and freethinking than sheep. This view of Americans has surfaced now and again in the course of our brief 200-year history as a nation. But fortunately we have an unblemished track record of seeing such a viewpoint backfire on the beholder. And more often than not, our communi-

cations media themselves have engineered the reversal, usually by exposing malfeasance in one or another of the key institutions in the country.

Television does, indeed, have a profound impact. It has been estimated that by the time the average high school student is graduated, he has logged about 20,000 hours in front of the tube—well over the amount of time he has spent in twelve years of school, homework excluded.

One good barometer of the intensity of this relationship is the fact that NBC hears from 250,000 to 300,000 viewers a year. Though many of these communications are by telephone, the bulk, about 70 percent, is in writing. So by going through the network mailbag for the last half-dozen years, one can get a good impression of the kinds of things that concern people "out there in TV land."

When shadows appeared on the lunar landscape during the Armstrong-Aldrin moon walk, some people "saw" things. Among the things people saw and called the network about were: a fifteen-foot-tall Russian lurking there, a Kodiak bear, and God. Said one anxious viewer: "Warn the astronauts immediately that they are in danger . . . they're not alone up there." A surprising number of viewers thought the whole show was a hoax, an audiovisual conspiracy engineered by the network in cahoots with the federal government. Concluded one cynic: "The entire event is being staged somewhere in Arizona." Still other viewers saw a different kind of conspiracy: to pipe illicit sex into the American home surreptitiously: "I found my children with their eyes glued to the TV laughing and giggling at that disgusting exhibition put on during the moon flight. That docking display was no more than a glorified show of two machines having sexual intercourse in space. How dare you!! I have young children to protect from such vulgarity. . . . I can no longer think up answers to my children's questions about 'docking.' "

Other viewers see shows that are not there at all. An NBC documentary on Saturday-night specials (handguns), *A Shooting Gallery Called America,* had been scheduled for airing in March, 1975. Any show on guns or hunting can be counted on to raise the hackles of gun enthusiasts, the "guns 'n' ammo" lobby. When the show was postponed, quite a few people nevertheless "saw" the special on guns and wrote in.

"We found it to be nothing more than a rehash of the same tired old theme: blaming the instrument, not the criminal."

"The Special 'A Shooting Gallery' was very informative and I would like to see it again."

As might be imagined, NBC's decision to show *The Godfather* in prime time created quite a bit of flak, and the network received 1,387 letters of protest in advance. Most of the mail was the result of an editorial in a Southern Baptist Convention publication that said, in part: "*The Godfather* elicits sympathy for some underworld people who make violence a way of life . . . TV violence does cause some people to act violently. To say that TV does not influence behavior is utterly foolish."

After all the initial ruckus, it turned out that many viewers had quite different concerns altogether. Some felt it had been too heavily "censored" for television and that too much had been edited out. Actually only fifty-four seconds were cut from the film, mostly in trimming some of the more gory close-ups. But the biggest beef was the scheduling: Saturday and Monday evenings:

"Like thousands of other second shift workers, I'm at home Saturday and Sunday but not Monday. Couldn't you show a 2-part movie either on Saturday and Sunday or two Saturdays?"

There are many "lobbies" in television land, though for the most part they are not organized formally like the pressure groups in Washington, D.C., that attempt to influence the government. One big lobby consists of sports fans. Like the "guns 'n' ammo" crowd, they are a very hard-nosed lot and do not want anything, repeat anything, interfering with their programs. But occasionally that happens. When it does, sports fans can be counted on to go bonkers. At NBC the classic example is still remembered as "the Heidi affair." The "incident" (to sports fans it was a national calamity) occurred on November 17, 1968. Pro football fans all across the country were glued to the tube avidly watching the final seconds of a tight game between the New York Jets and the Oakland Raiders. Though the Jets were ahead, there was just enough time left for the Raiders to turn the game around. At exactly 7 P.M., after the commercial break, a children's special, *Heidi*, which had been scheduled for that time, began. Sports fans looked on in complete disbelief, and rushed for the telephone. Then came the flood of letters, prompted in large part by the fact that the Raiders managed to score twice and beat the Jets.

"I am an avid pro football fan. You can have my wife (don't tell her), my automobile, my boat, but don't mess with my pro football games."

"My husband became so upset and distressed that I feared he would have a stroke, and I not only feared for his life but also the life of the television set . . ."

"NBC stands for 'No ballgames completed,' 'nothing but clods.' You should Heidi your face in shame."

"At this point I would like to tell you what you can do with your station, your AFL contract and dear old *Heidi* but I don't use that kind of language. Yours lovingly."

A great many fans did, indeed, use "that kind of language." But the reaction was not completely adverse, by any means. The network also heard from several thousand pro-*Heidi* folks:

"The children and I had been footballed to death . . ."

"I have three children who are perplexed week after week when football preempts their programs."

Aside from such mishaps, the sports fans usually have their way, particularly if the event is of major importance. This distresses the "antis" even more, a feeling that was crystallized with startling intensity in the spring of 1973 when the *final* episode of the much-admired *Alistair Cooke's America* series was washed out by a National Hockey League Stanley Cup playoff game. Some 8,400 irate viewers checked in.

Sports fans don't always win, though, because in the pecking order at the network, NBC News is Number One and can preempt any other department at any time if the occasion warrants.

Daytime drama fans form another big lobby. Though they may not be quite as hard-nosed or profane as are sports fans, they are just as dedicated to their particular national pastime and become acutely disturbed by any interruption. When the flight of *Apollo XV* preempted *Days of Our Lives* in the summer of 1971, many rebelled. "*Regular programs are far more important than trips to the moon—a dead old planet with nothing but rocks and dust.*"

But if the occasional preemption of one or another show

angers its devotees, the prospect that a favorite program might go off the air entirely really makes people angry. That includes children.

"Don't crumble this letter. I am 13 and I baby sit a lot for my nephew . . . a 15-month-old that likes to drive me *nuts*. I sit a lot on Saturday and I hear you're taking off the Andy Williams show . . . If you won't reconsider then how about you coming over here and baby sit for Alan. *You* put away the Jello when he throws it all over the floor. *You* clean up the pots and pans he throws around when he has nothing else to do. *You* clean up the dog food when he eats half of it and throws the other half around because he can't watch TV."

Once in a while the fans of a particular show are so devotedly wedded to it that they simply cannot accept the fact that it has gone off the air. When *The Monkees* was cancelled it drew a lot of protests, 153,479 of them! When *Star Trek* was scrubbed, there were 126,518 howls, somewhat below *The Monkees* mail. However, *Star Trek* fans are *different*. They *still* protest and have been doing so ever since the show went off, so that the ultimate protest count should top anything in television history. They seem to have a bumper sticker in their minds that reads: STAR TREK LIVES! Many of them are college students and graduates who have watched repeats four, five, even as many as eight times. And for the most part, they are articulate about why they like *Star Trek*.

"Star Trek has a powerfully dramatic message about the future of the human race. It shows a brotherhood of nations cooperating, clearly mankind's only hope."

"Star Trek . . . Just take a moment first to really meditate on the title . . . Really meditate on it. You'll see the light."

Whatever the individual response, to whatever show or issue, it is evident that the American public has an intense day-in, day-out relationship with television. Though most of NBC's mail is spontaneous, occasionally a write-in campaign is promoted. Usually such campaigns express a genuine concern, most often on the part of groups with a somewhat fundamentalist religious persuasion. In one instance, broadsides protesting the "low moral tone" of programs like *Rowan & Martin's Laugh-In* and *The Dean Martin Show* were widely circulated, along with enclosed postcards expressing protest, to be signed and sent in. The broadsides also solicited financial support for the campaign. For a period of time NBC received these cards at a rate of about 5,000 a week, and the total count ultimately climbed to over 100,000 cards.

Given the intense national involvement with television, coupled with strongly divergent views on what is appropriate air fare, broadcasters walk a fine and vigilant line in their efforts to produce programming that is genuinely in the public interest. Of all the preemptions, interruptions, and program cancellations that have either angered or pleased viewers, nothing in NBC's history ever fractured the *whole* of the vast audience quite like "the Watergate affair." Though it did not appear so at the time, the keynote speech that opened the Watergate saga was given on November 13, 1969, by then Vice-President Spiro Agnew. In that speech, Agnew proclaimed that the television news was biased and that it was slanted along liberal lines by the "Eastern establishment" which, he said, controls the networks. Clearly Agnew was speaking out in behalf of that segment of the American population so cherished by the Nixon White House, the "silent majority." One base-line idea was that the "vocal minority," namely those who were protesting the Vietnam war at the time, was receiving an undue amount of attention and air time compared to the silent majority which, presumably, supported the war. Therefore, the news was biased. It is, of course, true that journalists tend to cover things that are happening (demonstrations, for example) as opposed to things that are *not* happening (war supporters sitting home watching the demonstrations on TV). But by the same token one could say that a news item on a fire in a big apartment house should be balanced by a second item on the building next door, which did not catch fire. This problem of balance in the news has always plagued both television and the press, but we have to believe that in a free society such imbalances are generally restored over the long run. It quickly turned out that the silent majority was not that silent after all, once it had something to focus on. NBC alone received nearly 70,000 responses to the speech, 51,846 in favor of Agnew, 17,542 supporting the network. Spiro Agnew had touched a nerve that would continue to twinge as Watergate unraveled. That process began in the spring of 1973 with the Senate Select Committee's hearings, guided by Senator Sam Ervin, who became something of a Constitutional folk hero. The unraveling, and the television coverage thereof, grew in intensity throughout that year and into the next, topping out in the summer of 1974 with the Judiciary Committee hearings on impeachment and, in August, President Nixon's resignation. Early on, most protests involved the preemption of favorite shows. But as it became evident to the public that the hearings were destined to grind out over a long and almost inevitable course, some viewers, following up on Agnew's line of thought, felt that it was the media who were out to "get" the President, and others thought quite the opposite:

"Your newsmen revel in their broadcasts about Watergate."

"Unpatriotic acts like yours will destroy our form of Government."

"I don't think you can emphasize enough the seriousness of Watergate. Thank God for the news media!"

"We appreciate and love dearly our right to know. Please do not bow to the Administration's attacks."

As time passed, public opinion, at least as reflected in NBC's mail, turned increasingly in favor of covering the proceedings—probably because people became more and more aware that these were momentous times in American history. In any case, the public's confidence in television news and the press, which had slumped in 1972 in the Harris Survey mentioned earlier, no doubt due in large measure to Agnew's bias charges, rose to its new high in 1973 at the height of the affair and has continued to rise.

Much of the content of the letters and calls to NBC, about 35 percent, involves complaints and gripes of various sorts, which is to be expected. Yet, a surprising 15 percent contains praise for one program or another, surprising because satisfied viewers are the least inclined to communicate. But the majority of the comments, about half, concern quite different matters: requests for information, suggestions, and general comment. A sampling of these reveals that most people expect a lot from a TV network, even, on occasion, the miraculous. For example, there are those who hope NBC can provide dating services:

"Last Thursday or Friday I saw a piece on NBC about women garbage collectors or scavengers. I only saw 3 seconds of it. One was shapely. I would like to write to her."

"I am looking for a girl that was on a tv commercial as an Easter rabbit in 1970. This is an emergency. I must locate this girl at once. . ."

Then there are other kinds of requests:

"We are studying Frog Wars. We have heard that there is a Chinese belief on Frog Wars. If you have any information on Frog Wars, please send it to us."

"Hi! I'm doing a school report on endangered animals and I picked elephants. I saw your special you did and wondered if you could send me some."

"While enjoying the half-time program of the UCLA-Notre Dame basketball game I realized I had never seen a picture of the Great Wall of China suitable for framing. Do you have one . . ."

As is to be expected, there are many aspiring actresses and actors out there:

"I would like to know if you are having auditishins for an 11 year old boy . . . I can do imitations of people such as Richard Nixin, Howard cosel . . ."

"I would like to add my 2¢. Television is run down at the heels. What you need is a top performer. I am such! People like my style and are after me to do a show. Call me. P.S. People with my ability command top price."

People also have ideas to offer:

"I have a friend that has a gumpaper chain over 100 ft. long. Theres about 25 different kinds of gumpapers like grape or spearmint. She may have set a new world record or made one. It would be neat for your news."

"I would like to suggest a program where once a month two reporters would review the passing away of famous people. Call it 'Passing On.' "

There are queries, too:

"On the NBC news Senator Hartke said he would like to turn this country around. Is there any way you can find out where I will be located?"

"I admire George Peppard's hair style—it is one that could be adapted to meet my particular needs and facial contours. Does the style have a technical name? This might be of assistance . . ."

"In Sanford and Son, is the son a white man or a black man in real life?"

"What is the heartbeat of a whale? We are studying it in Science. Do you know if Moby Dick is still alive?"

Finally, there is a continuous flow of comment:

" 'In Search of Ancient Astronauts' did not convince me that the prehistoric earth was visited by spacemen, but it did make me wonder whether intelligent life exists at NBC."

"Here in Fonda, Iowa, we had streaking long before it hit the headlines. Around the time of World War I, on a hot summer's night one Max Evans, now deceased, streaked through our town playing the violin. He had greased his body and it was only by putting on cloth gloves that his captors succeeded in collaring him. The citizens of Fonda, Iowa, demand that the public know we were ahead by more than fifty years. Fonda though small (pop. 980) has always been progressive."

"I just wanted you to know how wonderful I think your newsmen are—I *love* Jim Hartz, I *love* Chuck Scarborough, I *adore* John Chancellor. I think they're simply superfluous!"

There is no doubt at all that the American people have developed an intense relationship with television, one that can be highly emotional at times, depending on one or another viewer's particular concerns or interests. And since the medium is so all-pervasive in our society, it is easy to imagine that it must be "doing something" to us in ways we can only imagine. This makes it very tempting for some to regard television as a "sinister force" and to speculate as to what its sinister effects might be. Are the microwaves that fill the air today somehow programming our brains? Is television turning America into a nation of think-alike, homogenized beings? Is it destroying literacy? Is it exhorting the young to violence? Is it somehow "liberalizing" people against their will via an "Eastern establishment" bias in the news?

A list of such questions could go on almost indefinitely. It may be tempting to ask such questions, but it has to be noted that the concern that such questions arise from is not unique to the era of television. It has arisen whenever a new medium of communication has taken on widespread appeal. In radio days, people worried that those presuppertime shows that held kids spellbound were "doing something" to them. Before World War II, comic books were alleged to be a "sinister force," evoking violence in the young. In the 1930s, there was considerable concern that Hollywood movies were corrupting our morals. And way back at the turn of the century, there was a hue and cry about "penny dreadfuls," cheap magazinelike illustrated books, featuring lurid shoot-'em-up stories by writers like Ned Buntline (for whom Samuel Colt created the famous long-barreled six-shooter, the "Buntline Special"). Hundreds of years ago, the introduction of movable type was regarded with suspicion by an elite who felt that it opened new areas that were dangerous to the human mind.

All of these worries were based on pure speculation. There is no hard evidence that such concerns were warranted—in fact, in some instances, the concerns were completely unfounded. This is not to say that such questions are not worth asking or pursuing. But to determine the effects of television on the American people, we need solid data, not fanciful speculations, and we are likely to find that television has different effects on different people. Television is a mass medium, serving a number of diverse "publics," and it tends to be conservative (unlike some feature motion pictures and theatrical offerings). And there *is* evidence that the viewing audience reflects this conservatism.

If what television is doing *to* us is a matter of speculation, what it is doing *for* us certainly is not. It is surely a blessing to many, many elderly people who have little else to enjoy in life. It provides sports fans with the best seat in the house for a host of major events, few of which they would be able to watch in person. For housewives, and for many others as well, it offers games and dramas to liven up a day's routine. It has introduced young people to all sorts of experiences they might very well otherwise have missed, including the wonders of many of the more exotic realms of the natural world. It offers comedy and variety, drama and the movies, for everyone. And it has made the American people the best-informed population on earth.

But such specifics are only a pale reflection of the real impact of television. Today, for the first time in history, several hundred million people have easy access to the whole world and even, on occasion, to the depths of space. Today, for the first time in our history, we have instant access to one another. Today, the once-isolated privileged, and the equally isolated inner-city poor, meet one another—on television. The same applies to all sorts of other groups: farmers and students, housewives and firemen, bus drivers and businessmen, storekeepers and hustlers, factory workers and environmentalists, politicians and civil servants—the list is endless, just as the diversity of America is. And television reflects it all. Like the slowly turning mirrored ball in a dance hall, television reflects all the corners of America and all its people, to each individual who watches. Far from being a sinister force, it is a cohesive one, a force that mirrors our land and ourselves, our problems and our needs, and those of the world beyond as well. At no time was this cohesion clearer than on the days surrounding the assassination of President Kennedy. Television held us together and helped assure us that an orderly transfer of authority was taking place.

In accomplishing the somewhat incredible feat of making a whole nation visible to itself, television has had a profound impact on politics. Today, particularly at the state and national levels, any candidate becomes highly visible to the whole electorate, and each person watching can make an individual judgment on the contender's merits.

On the cultural level it is easy to put television down as a wasteland. It is, after all, a commercial enterprise. And there are many different audiences to be considered, each with its own expectations. Balancing such varied interests is a continuing challenge as more and more people tune in for increasingly longer times. The result is never perfect, all interests are never fully satisfied, and programming continually changes in an effort to keep an attractive balance. Yet who would have thought, even a generation ago, that tens of millions of people would be able to watch a first-rate production, in color, of *Jane Eyre* or *The Red Badge of Courage,* or visit the Louvre or the Kremlin, or float leisurely down the Nile or the Colorado, or have the best seat in the house for the Super Bowl or national conventions, or explore the undersea world with Jacques Cousteau or step out on the moon with Neil Armstrong, or then look back for an exquisite view of Spaceship Earth drifting in the blackness of space? It really is, as Bob Hope says at the beginning of this book, simply amazing.

The publisher wishes to acknowledge gratefully the help offered by the following people:
Charlie Andrews, Marvin Antonowsky, Curt Block, Milton Brown, Dean Craig, Les Crystal, Fred deCordova, Marilyn Deen, Sid Desfor, Dick Ebersol, Til Ferdenzi, Reuven Frank, George Heinemann, Bettye Hoffmann, Bill Hogan, Bob Hope, Roy Huggins, Rick Kelly, Jim Kitchell, Richard Levinson, William Link, William R. McAndrew, Jr., William J. McGuire, J. Ronald Milavsky, Robert O'Neil, Betty Jane Reed, Joe Riccuiti, Hank Rieger, Stanley Rotkewicz, Stuart Schulberg, Doug Sinsel, Jerry Stanley, Bill Stein, Bill Storke, Joe Taritero, David Tebet, Jack Tracy, Mike Weinblatt, Mort Werner

and special thanks also to:
Bob Abel, Carol Aerenson, Sigmund Bajak, Joe Bernstein, Hugh M. Beville, Jr., Joe Bleeden, Sil Carinchini, Johnny Carson, John Chancellor, Carolyn Churchill, Fenton Coe, Owen Comora, Barbara Cooper, Betty Corday, William Danhauser, Madeline David, Eddie Deep, Henni Dowenfeld, Doug Duitsman, Dick Edmondson, Denise Elliott, Nancy Fields, Norm Frisch, Greg Garrison, David Gerber, Richard Harper Graham, Ward Grant, John Hamlin, Joyce Hunt, Sam Kaufman, Jack Kennedy, Bryna P. Laub, Cathy Lim, Carl Lindemann, Walter Lord, Steward MacGregory, John J. McMahon, Helen Manasian, Mary Mark, Perry Massey, Vera Mayer, Leonard Meyers, Lorne Michaels, Sheldon Nemeyer, Linda Oken, Al Perlmutter, Virginia E. Pike, Al Pinsky, Al Rabin, Bill Rubens, Sharron Sampson, Tom Sarnoff, Art Selby, Gene Shalit, Les Slater, Mike Smith, Peter Tintle, Gene Walsh, Dick Welsch

All photographs courtesy NBC except for those on pages 105 (*bottom*), 107, and 108, which are by Allan Price.